Why Jesus Matters

Why Jesus Matters

George W. Stroup

WJK Westminster John Knox Press
Louisville • Kentucky

A revision and updating of *Jesus Christ for Today*
(Westminster Press, 1982)

Published by Westminster John Knox Press
Louisville, Kentucky

11 12 13 14 15 16 17 18 19 20—10 9 8 7 6 5 4 3 2 1

Book design by Sharon Adams
Cover design by Pam Poll Graphic Design
Cover art © Design Pics/iStockphoto.com

Library of Congress Cataloging-in-Publication Data

Stroup, George W., 1944–
Why Jesus matters / George W. Stroup.—1st ed.
p. cm.
ISBN 978-0-664-23461-4 (alk. paper)
1. Jesus Christ—Person and offices. I. Stroup, George W., 1944– Jesus Christ for Today. II. Title.
BT203.S86 2011
232'.8—dc22

2010034962

PRINTED IN THE UNITED STATES OF AMERICA

♾ The paper used in this publication meets the minimum requirements of the American National Standard for Information Sciences—Permanence of Paper for Printed Library Materials, ANSI Z39.48-1992.

Westminster John Knox Press advocates the responsible use of our natural resources. The text paper of this book is made from at least 30% postconsumer waste.

Contents

Preface

Why Jesus Matters is a revision of my book *Jesus Christ for Today*, first published by Westminster Press in 1982 in their Library of Living Faith series, edited by John M. Mulder. In his foreword to those ten volumes, Mulder explains that the series is an attempt to continue the Layman's Theological Library, a very successful series of books Westminster Press had published in the 1950s.

This history is significant because it says something about the intent of *Why Jesus Matters*. It is written not for professional theologians but for "laity," for Christians who do not necessarily have formal theological education but who are interested in thinking about important theological topics in Christian faith. There is no theological topic more important for Christian faith than Christology.

This volume has two purposes. First, it tries to explain why Christology is truly so important. Second, it tries to explain why professional theologians continue to write books about Jesus. What is it about Jesus that prompts theologians across the centuries to continue writing books about him? The answer to that question is the original title of this book, which was taken from a comment by the German theologian Dietrich Bonhoeffer in *Letters and Papers from Prison*, written at the end of the Second World War as he sat in a Nazi prison, awaiting his execution.

"What is bothering me incessantly," Bonhoeffer says, "is the question what Christianity really is, or indeed who Christ really is, for us today." Bonhoeffer's question reflects Jesus' question to his disciples in Mark 8:29, "But who do you say that I am?" Theologians keep writing books about Jesus because he is a living Christ who continues to ask each new generation of Christians who they believe him to be.

Jesus Christ for Today was published almost thirty years ago, so the "us" in "Who is Jesus Christ for us today?" is different. Those of us who were asking that question then are now different, and our world is significantly different. I think that is one reason why the Editorial Board at Westminster John Knox Press asked me to revise the original book. I have restructured the book, omitted some of the material in the original volume, and added new material in an attempt to do two things. First, I have tried to indicate a few of the important developments in the discussion of Christology that have taken place since 1982. Most of those are included in chapter 5. Second, Christology in the last decades of the twentieth century has been influenced by the emergence of new proposals from theologians in the non-Western world and by interreligious dialogue with people from other faiths. Chapter 6 briefly addresses both of these developments.

In the spirit of Jesus' question to his disciples at Caesarea Philippi in Mark 8, the Editorial Board of Westminster John Knox Press also asked me to rewrite the book as a response to questions often asked about Jesus Christ. I am grateful to my friend Don McKim of the Editorial Board for that request and for thinking that the original volume is worth rewriting and republishing. I am also grateful for his encouragement and patience as I missed deadline after deadline.

The volume on Jesus Christ in the original Layman's Theological Library was titled *The Meaning of Christ* and was written by Robert Clyde Johnson, Professor of Theology and Dean of Yale Divinity School. Bob Johnson was a fine theologian, dean, and pastor. Forty years ago he was my teacher and taught me to love theology. This book is dedicated to his memory.

Chapter One

Does Christ Matter?

Could There Be a Church without Christ?

The question may seem absurd at first, perhaps even silly. The very name "Christianity," after all, presupposes "Christ." How could there be such a thing as Christianity without Christ? Obviously Christ matters to Christians. Otherwise they would not call themselves "Christians." And Christ may even be of interest to non-Christians who are curious about Christianity, in the same way that Christians interested in Islam are curious about Muhammad.

Is it possible to imagine Christianity without Christ? The novelist Flannery O'Connor thought so. In her novel *Wise Blood*, O'Connor tells the story of Hazel Motes, a preacher of the Church Without Christ. "Well, I preach the Church Without Christ. I'm member and preacher to that church where the blind don't see and the lame don't walk and what's dead stays that way. Ask me about that church and I'll tell you it's the church that the blood of Jesus don't foul with redemption."[1] That may strike us as both humorous and bizarre, as O'Connor intended, but Hazel Motes's understanding of the gospel is no more bizarre than many others today. There are as many views of Jesus as there are interpretations of Christianity and the gospel, since the two are not necessarily synonymous. In many cases "Jesus" simply serves to bolster values and commitments that have little or nothing to do with the New Testament. What really matters is a church's warm hospitality or its advocacy of particular social and political values—liberal or conservative—or its promise that it can help its members gain wealth, prosperity, and respectability. More often than not, when these things are at the heart of a church's life, "Jesus" is simply the means by which they are "baptized" and given the veneer of Christian values. These things tell us more about that particular church than they do about Jesus. Rarely is Jesus allowed to challenge and reinterpret a church's understanding of hospitality, politics, and abundance.

Many Christians use "Jesus" and "Christ" interchangeably or as though Christ were Jesus' surname, but that is a serious mistake. The theologian Paul Tillich preferred to speak of "Jesus the Christ" in order to make it clear that Christ, derived from the Greek word for Messiah, is a title attributed to Jesus and is not his family name.[2] Additionally, for reasons we will discuss throughout this book, many Christians today are more comfortable with the Christ than they are with Jesus. People find something intellectually offensive about the particularity of Christian claims that the very reality of God, the Word, was embodied in a first-century Jew in a remote corner of the Roman Empire. And so they should. It is easier to talk about something more general, more abstract, like the Messiah, than it is the specific person, Jesus of Nazareth. The idea of the Christ is more attractive than the historical reality that is Jesus of Nazareth.

This reticence that some Christians have regarding Jesus may be a sign he is not as central to their faith as they think. Many people in so-called mainline Protestant churches have difficulty talking about him. Although referred to frequently in the preaching, liturgy, hymns, and prayers of the church and in its official statements of belief and mission, many Christians are uncertain what they want to say about Jesus. They are more at ease talking about community, hospitality, peace, and justice. Ask members of an adult Sunday school class in almost any mainline denomination what role Jesus plays in their understanding of themselves and how they live their daily lives: you are likely to hear nothing but an awkward, embarrassed silence. No doubt there are many reasons for this widespread reticence. Some people have heard or read about Christians who talk about Jesus in ways that reflect a piety and an understanding of the world that sounds otherworldly and unrelated to daily experience. Others worry that they may embarrass themselves by "saying the wrong thing" about Jesus. They may know that their church has creeds and confessions that make important claims about Jesus, but they probably have never understood what those statements mean. Their ministers may have a theological education and may understand these theological claims about Jesus, but these other members do not. They sense that they do not know the appropriate (and inappropriate) things to say about Jesus, and rather than embarrass themselves, they prefer to say nothing at all. Many people today are simply tongue-tied when asked to talk about Jesus.

So is it possible to imagine a Church Without Christ? Perhaps it is difficult to imagine a church publically and officially renouncing its faith in Jesus, but given the difficulty that many Christians have in talking about Jesus and the role he plays (or does not play) in their lives, it may not be as bizarre as it first appears. What would a Church Without Christ look like? What would be the consequences for Christian faith if Jesus Christ were peripheral? The church might well endure. Its rituals, worship, and life might continue. Jesus might recede into the background, like a fondly remembered deceased uncle, but Wednesday night church suppers would continue unabated.

Who Is Jesus Christ for Us Today?

This question whether Jesus is really necessary for Christian faith presupposes two others: Who *was* Jesus? Who *is* Jesus? Who was that person sometimes referred to as "the historical Jesus," the Jesus who lived in Galilee in the first third of the first century? And who is this same Jesus for people living not in the first century, but in the twenty-first? "Jesus Christ" or "Jesus the Christ" refers to Jesus of Nazareth, who his followers believed to be Israel's long-awaited and hoped-for Messiah, who would establish

God's kingdom on earth. Although many figures before Jesus were thought to be the Messiah (and some made claims to be so), when Christians talk about Christ, they are referring to one, particular person: a first-century Jew named Jesus from the small town of Nazareth in Galilee. So who was this Jesus, and why did first-century Jews give him the title of "Christ" or "Messiah"?

We will discuss the historical Jesus in chapter 2, but before doing so it is important to remember that the question of Jesus' identity is seldom asked with disinterest. The question usually carries considerable baggage because most people know that traditionally Christians refer to Jesus as the Christ because they believe him to be their savior and redeemer. Therefore, the question as to the identity of the historical Jesus is often tangled up with the question of why Christians call him the Christ. History and faith are closely intertwined. Why do they believe him to be their savior and redeemer? This is not a new question but a perennial one that was asked in the first century and continues to be asked today. It goes to the heart of the meaning of Christian faith and will probably continue to be asked as long as people, both Christians and non-Christians, inquire into the significance of the gospel. This book explores these questions and some of the ways in which the Christian community has answered them.

Since the first century, Christians have heard these questions about Jesus of Nazareth asked in different forms and for different reasons. Some churches have tried to answer them by means of creeds and confessions, perhaps the best known of which are the Apostles' Creed and the Nicene Creed. On the basis of the witness of Scripture and its claims about Jesus, early Christians wrote these theological statements in order publically to confess their faith that Jesus is the Christ and is Lord and Savior of the world. They tried to make their claims about him consistent with what they thought was in the Bible, their primary resource, and with their experience of him in worship and in their daily lives. In addition to these ancient creeds, Christians have continued to confess their faith in Jesus in ways that reflect new issues and questions unknown to their predecessors. It is this latter consideration—that what churches say about Christian faith should be responsive and intelligible to their contemporary setting—that makes theological reflection about Jesus Christ both terribly difficult and extremely important.

Many Christians have long recognized the importance of being faithful to the witness of Scripture and of being guided and instructed by the faith and experience of previous generations. Yet they also understand that what they say about Christian faith in general and Jesus Christ in particular must be intelligible to the world in which they live. Consequently they have been unwilling simply to repeat ancient creeds and confessions in response to new questions asked about Jesus Christ. Churches continue to confess their faith in him, but they do so differently than early Christians did in order to make the gospel intelligible and compelling in their new historical and cultural contexts. For example, the Nicene Creed, written in the early fourth century, describes Jesus as "the only-begotten Son of God, begotten of the Father before all worlds, God of God, Light of Light, Very God of Very God, begotten, not made, being of one substance with the Father, by whom all things were made."[3] This language made New Testament claims about Jesus intelligible to Christians living in fourth-century Mediterranean culture.

On the other hand, a more recent confessional statement by the Presbyterian Church (U.S.A.), the Confession of 1967, uses quite different language. It emphasizes the humanity and ministry of Jesus Christ, themes ignored by the Nicene Creed. It declares that

> Jesus, a Palestinian Jew, lived among his own people and shared their needs, temptations, joys, and sorrows. He expressed the love of God in word and deed and became a brother to all kinds of sinful men. But his complete obedience led him into conflict with his people. His life and teaching judged their goodness, religious aspirations, and national hopes. Many rejected him and demanded his death. In giving himself freely for them, he took upon himself the judgment under which all men stand convicted. God raised him from the dead, vindicating him as Messiah and Lord.[4]

These two theological statements about Jesus Christ are separated by over sixteen hundred years, and yet one of them is not necessarily "better" or more truthful than the other. Each must be understood in its historical, theological, and cultural context. Each tries to make claims about Jesus Christ in a different context—the Nicene Creed in the early fourth century, when the known world was limited to the Mediterranean Sea, Western Europe, and what was once called Asia Minor; and the Confession of 1967, in the mid-twentieth century, when humans for the first time set foot on the moon. The first describes Jesus as "of one substance with the Father" while the other claims that Jesus was a Palestinian Jew who "expressed the love of God in word and deed." These are two quite different descriptions of Jesus. Why are they so different?

Christians have never believed that the central reality of their faith—the grace of God in Jesus Christ—is only an artifact in a museum of religious history. Rather, this God who has been disclosed in Jesus of Nazareth is a living reality who continues to speak to people and to be active in the world. Christians are called and commissioned to listen for God's Word, which addresses them anew in the living Christ. Therefore the church cannot be faithful to this God simply by repeating old confessions: the church must continue to listen for what God's graceful yet disturbing Word in Jesus Christ calls them to do in their contemporary world.

Perhaps it was this conviction that led the German theologian and martyr Dietrich Bonhoeffer to write from his prison cell on April 30, 1944, "What is bothering me incessantly is the question what Christ really is, or indeed who Christ really is, for us today."[5] Bonhoeffer did not ask that question out of ignorance of what early Christians had said about Jesus Christ or out of despair that Jesus Christ was no longer significant for Christians in Germany in the midst of the Second World War. He asked that question because he believed that God continues to address the world through Jesus Christ and that Christians must attend to this living Christ if they are to be faithful to the gospel they confess and the God they worship.

Is Jesus Christ the Center of Christian Faith?

Bonhoeffer's question What is Christianity, and who is Jesus Christ for us today? deserves serious reflection. It points to what Christians have recognized for a long time: the meaning of the gospel is inseparable from Jesus of Nazareth. This Jesus gives Christian faith its distinctive meaning and shape. Christian faith apart from him—Hazel Motes's Church Without Christ—bears no resemblance to the good news described in the New Testament. In order to answer the question "What is the gospel?" churches through the ages have pointed to Jesus Christ and what God has done in and through him. Second, Bonhoeffer reminds us that, although Christians throughout history are united by their common confession that "Jesus is Lord," the lordship of Christ may mean quite different things in different times and places. Christians believe that Jesus Christ is always "for us"—"If God is for us, who is against us?" (Romans 8:31)—but the sense in which he is for us and what his call to discipleship means cannot be determined apart from specific contexts. Christ does not call people to discipleship in general. He calls particular people to their particular crosses and to specific forms of discipleship.

Christian faith affirms that the meaning of life is found in a relationship to that ultimate reality known as "God," a reality that encounters people in the person of a first-century Jew named Jesus. In him people come to know God to be gracious, loving, and faithful. Jesus of Nazareth, therefore, is the center of Christian faith—the basis for what Christians believe they know about God. Jesus is the reason Christians believe they are called to lead lives that witness to the grace and love of God. Jesus is the basis for their hope that God is faithful even when they are not, and the reason they trust that the future belongs to God and is to be anticipated with confidence rather than despair.

Christian faith can be compared to a prism. Just as a single prism has many facets, so too there are many different but related convictions that make up Christian faith. At an intellectual level these different facets are called "doctrines." Jesus Christ is the light that passes through the prism of Christian faith and enables Christians to see the meaning of realities such as God's love and grace, creation, sin, forgiveness, church, and God's kingdom. Jesus is the light that allows Christians to see what these things are in themselves and in their relation to one another. For example, the apostle Paul insists that the church in its most important sense is "the body of Christ" (1 Corinthians 12:12–31). Theologically that means that it is not the church that helps Christians understand who Jesus is, but that Jesus is the one who tells them what the church is and what it is called to do in the world.

But while Jesus of Nazareth may be the central reality for how Christians understand God and life in response to God's grace in Jesus Christ, Jesus has been and continues to be an elusive figure, for both Christians and non-Christians alike. Jesus has been understood in many different ways by Christians through the centuries, and that is no less true today. Jesus has many "faces" in our contemporary world. Christians who belong to conservative religious and political movements in the United States often describe Jesus in ways that stress the sanctity of the individual, the value of human life (yet allowing for war and capital punishment), the importance of the right to own a gun, and the evils of moral behavior that deviates from the norms of middle-class society. On the other hand, some Christian communities in Latin America and other parts of the non-Western world describe a very different Jesus: one who takes the side of the poor and oppressed in their struggle against oppressive and unjust social policies and institutions. Their Jesus calls Christians to participate in the struggle against social oppression in order that they may give a witness to the meaning of the cross and the coming of God's kingdom. Christians of a conservative religious and political persuasion point to texts in the New Testament such as Jesus' claim that "My kingdom is not from this world" (John 18:36) and his admonition "Do not work for the food that perishes, but for the food that endures for eternal life, which the Son of Man will give you" (John 6:27). Christians sympathetic to liberation movements point to different biblical texts, such as the one in Matthew in which Jesus describes a day of judgment when the Son of Man will separate people on the basis of their response to him:

> Then he will say to those at his left hand, "You that are accursed, depart from me into the eternal fire prepared for the devil and his angels; for I was hungry and you gave me no food, I was thirsty and you gave me nothing to drink, I was a stranger and you did not welcome me, naked and you did not give me clothing, sick and in prison and you did not visit me." Then they also will answer, "Lord, when was it that we saw you hungry or thirsty or a stranger or naked or sick or in prison, and did not take care of you?" Then he will answer them, "Truly I tell you, just as you did not do it to one of these least of these, you did not do it to me." And these will go away into eternal punishment, but the righteous into eternal life. (Matthew 25:41–46)

Both kinds of Christians quote the Bible.

To non-Christians, who merely observe what Christians say and do, it may be unclear how these two very different interpretations of Jesus of Nazareth refer to the same person. Not only are these two pictures of Jesus quite different, but because Jesus is the center of Christian faith, the interpretations of Christian faith and life that accompany them also differ significantly. Are these really two different interpretations of the same Jesus? Their differences appear to be so great that it is unclear to many people how they can both be described as "Christian." For some people these diverse pictures of Jesus raise the question of whether Jesus Christ really is the center of Christian faith or whether he is simply a prop for a faith that is based on a particular political ideology.

For four reasons, however, most Christians continue to insist that despite the many different ways in which Jesus is understood, he remains the central reality of Christian faith: first, Jesus allows people to see the true nature of God; second, Jesus Christ defines the meaning of salvation; third, he provides Christian individuals and communities with their true identity; and, fourth, he defines the nature and mission of the church.

Is Jesus God?

This is a simple question. Surely there must be a simple answer. Unfortunately not. Christian faith is earthy, this-worldly, specific, and particular. It is not a philosophy, a metaphysics, a worldview, or a moral system. It is rooted in the conviction that the sacred mystery that Christians refer to as "God" became visible in the person of Jesus of Nazareth and in the New Testament's stories about him. Christians do not believe their faith is a series of abstractions and generalities; they understand it to be read off the face and life of a specific person who lived in a particular time and place. The First Letter of John leaves no confusion about this:

> We declare to you what was from the beginning, what we have heard, what we have seen with our eyes, what we have looked at and touched with our hands, concerning the word of life—this life was revealed, and we have seen it and testify to it, and declare to you the eternal life that was with the Father and was revealed to us—we declare to you what we have seen and heard so that you also may have fellowship with us; and truly our fellowship is with the Father and with his Son Jesus Christ. (1 John 1:1–3)

The love of God is here neither an abstraction nor a generality. The claim that Christians should "love one another" (1 John 4:7) follows from the conviction that the reality of God has been heard, seen, looked upon, and touched in the person of Jesus of Nazareth. Jesus is the indispensable center of Christian faith because he is the specific, visible representation of God and God's love for the world. The technical term that Christians use to make this confession is "incarnation." In the language of John's Gospel, Jesus is the Word who "became flesh and lived among us" (John 1:14); he is literally the "embodiment" of God. This Jesus makes God's grace, love, and mercy a tangible, earthy reality.

Looking for the center of Christian faith somewhere else than in Jesus makes it less specific and more abstract than it is described in the New Testament. Why have Christians sometimes done that? Because there is something scandalous about Jesus' death by crucifixion, as Paul recognized in 1 Corinthians 1:18–31 (see v. 23, "stumbling block"). But the scandal of the gospel is not just the cross. It is also what some theologians have described as "the scandal of particularity"—the Christian claim that the full reality of that ineffable mystery that Christians refer to as "God" is embodied in a mid-first-century Jew from Nazareth in Galilee, a remote backwater village in the Roman Empire. Christians who do not stumble over that claim do not hear the shocking and outrageous message of the New Testament. One way to diffuse the offensiveness and scandal of that claim is to make the gospel about something other than Jesus of Nazareth—something more acceptable to contemporary sensibilities, such as love, peace, and tolerance. It is much easier to advocate an abstract notion of love than to advocate Jesus Christ crucified. Love in general is far more appealing because we can make it mean whatever we want. The suffering love of the cross that calls Christians to self-denying discipleship is not as attractive. Christian faith as described in the New Testament, however, is not an idea or a set of moral principles, but a person in whom Christians believe they encounter the full reality of God's grace and suffering love.

Although the incarnation is vitally important for understanding why Jesus of Nazareth is the center of Christian faith, it is possible to misinterpret the incarnation in ways that distort it. While Jesus of Nazareth is the center of Christian faith, he is not a second god or a substitute for God. In some Christian communities, Jesus is not only the embodiment of God; he also becomes the sole object of worship. It is one thing to say that the Word of God is heard and seen in Jesus of Nazareth, or to say with the apostle Paul that "in Christ God was reconciling the world to himself" (2 Corinthians 5:19). It is something else to reduce without remainder the Christian doctrine of the Trinity—the claim that God is one substance in three persons—to Jesus of Nazareth. When Jesus prays in Gethsemane, "Abba, Father, for you all things are possible;

remove this cup from me; yet not what I want, but what you want" (Mark 14:36), he is not talking to himself. In the New Testament the good news of Easter is that God raised Jesus from the dead, which is not the same thing as saying that Jesus raised himself.

While the Christian doctrine of the incarnation points to the unique and crucial importance of Jesus of Nazareth for understanding what Christians mean by "God," Christianity is not and must not be allowed to become what some theologians have colorfully described as "Jesusolatry." Jesus of Nazareth is "God with us" (Matthew 1:23) and the Word who "became flesh and lived among us" (John 1:14), the reality of God made visible and audible in human history; but Jesus is not a replacement for the full reality of the triune God. Jesus of Nazareth and the confession that he is Lord and Savior of the world (John 4:42) are the basis for the Christian claim that the one God of Deuteronomy 6:4 is three persons—Father, Son, and Holy Spirit. In human history, Jesus is the incarnation of the Son or Word of God, but it is the Father who sends the Son (John 3:16) and the Spirit who makes him present and enables people to have faith in him. Historically it was just these questions about the relation between Jesus and the one he addressed as "Abba" or "Father" that finally led the early church to formulate its understanding of God as triune. The doctrine of the Trinity affirms on the one hand that in the person of Jesus of Nazareth the world encounters the very reality of God, but on the other hand that the object of Christian worship is the triune God revealed in Jesus' life and ministry. It is not accidental that many churches embracing Jesusolatry have also purged any mention of the Trinity from their hymns and liturgy. Such a misrepresentation of Jesus' relation to the Trinity is contrary to the creeds and confessions of the early church.

Christians believe that Jesus of Nazareth is the visible representation of the reality of God, or to use a phrase made popular by contemporary theologians, Jesus is "the human face of God." It is the very human face of Jesus—a face that the New Testament nowhere describes—that is the basis for the specific, tangible, earthy understanding that Christians have of the grace and love of God.

So is Jesus God? Yes and No. Yes, Jesus is the embodiment of the very reality of the triune God, but no, Jesus is the Word made flesh and must not be confused with either the One he calls Abba or the Spirit he sends to his disciples, the Spirit who gives them the faith to believe in him.

Why Do Christians Call Jesus "Savior"?

Second, Jesus is the indispensable center of Christian faith not only because he is the basis for what Christians believe about God but also because he is the basis for their understanding of salvation. For many Christians, Paul's claim in 2 Corinthians 5:19 that "in Christ God was reconciling the world to himself" is a summary of the gospel. That text suggests two foci to Christian faith, both of which are necessary for an adequate interpretation of the gospel. On the one hand, as we have seen, faith confesses that the Word of God has become visible and audible in Jesus of Nazareth, but it became visible in Jesus of Nazareth for a purpose: in order that the world might be reconciled to God, or in the words of John 3:16, "so that everyone who believes in him may not perish but may have eternal life." If the incarnation is not understood in relation to what Christians mean by salvation and reconciliation, it becomes an interesting but finally irrelevant religious mystery. God's reconciliation of the world in Jesus Christ makes the incarnation relevant and meaningful.

Here we encounter one of the most important claims of Christian faith. We cannot understand who Jesus was and is unless we understand his significance for the world and for ourselves. At issue is the Christian conviction that the fundamental human problem is sin, and by "sin" Christians mean the corruption of the one relationship that is most important to all people: their relation to God. To not only sin but also to be "in sin," as all people are (for "all have sinned and fall short of the glory of God" [Romans 3:23]), is both to live in a world that is estranged from God and to engage in acts that further estrange people from both God and their neighbors.

In the life, death, and resurrection of Jesus Christ, Christians believe that God overcomes the brokenness of human sin and reconciles them to God and to one another. The technical term that Christians use to describe this "overcoming" is "atonement," and we discuss it in greater detail in chapter 3. Because Jesus is the Word made flesh and because of what he does, Christians believe they have a restored relation to God and to one another and are given a new life of faith, hope, and love. It was this conviction that led Philipp Melanchthon, a sixteenth-century Lutheran theologian, to argue that "to know Christ means to know his benefits."[6] He asked, "Unless you know why Christ put on flesh and was nailed to the cross, what good will it do you to know merely the history about him?"[7]

The Christian confession that "God was in Christ" gives salvation its distinctive shape, and most important, it declares that salvation, like God's love, is not an abstract idea but a reality in the midst of human history. As the Nicene Creed puts it, Christ "for us men, and for our salvation, came down from heaven, was incarnate by the Holy Spirit of the Virgin Mary, and was made man, and was crucified also for us under Pontius Pilate."[8] Salvation is particular, visible, and accessible to all people. The incarnation enables Christians to claim that God's gracious act of reconciliation has taken place in human history and includes the whole of God's creation (Colossians 1:15–20).

Not only is Jesus the basis for what Christians know about God; he also points to the distinctive feature of this knowledge, that it is "unto salvation." Hence, the knowledge of God that Christians have in Jesus Christ is a peculiar form of knowledge. It is not merely "objective," such as the knowledge that one might have about the distance between New York and Boston or the number of moons around Saturn, but knowledge that alters a person's understanding of their identity (who they are) and what kind of person they are. It is what some have described as "existential" knowledge: knowledge that alters one's understanding of self and world. Either what Christians claim about God on the basis of Jesus of Nazareth is not true and the gospel is not good news, or it is true and calls for the conversion and transformation of their lives. If what Christians claim to know about God is true, then that is not just one more piece of information that they can add to their trove of important data. To know God's grace and love in Jesus of Nazareth is also to experience transformation, to turn around, and to begin walking in a different direction, to discover that one is what the apostle Paul describes as "a new creation" (2 Corinthians 5:17).

When Christians read the New Testament's stories about Jesus, they believe they encounter the drama of God's redemption of the world. These stories include the whole of creation and yet are also intensely personal and world-transforming. Jesus is indispensable for understanding Christian faith because Christians believe that in him and in the stories that give him his identity they encounter a grace that redeems them from both personal and social forms of brokenness and calls them to a life of discipleship, which the New Testament refers to as a "ministry of reconciliation." Because Jesus of Nazareth is the basis for what Christians believe about God, so too Jesus defines how they understand love and freedom. Unfortunately these phrases—"Christian love" and "Christian freedom"—are used so often in the church and in contemporary culture that they have become religious platitudes and have lost their sting and their proper offensiveness. They have been domesticated by a Christian society whose structures and policies contradict what the New Testament means by sacrificial, self-giving love and a freedom that is obedience to God's call to covenant faithfulness. In contemporary culture, fiction often speaks the truth of Christian faith more clearly than the church does. In Flannery O'Connor's short story "A Good Man Is Hard to Find," an escaped convict, appropriately named The Misfit, speaks the truth moments before he murders an elderly grandmother:

> "Jesus was the only One that ever raised the dead," The Misfit continued, "and He shouldn't have done it. He thrown everything off balance. If He did what he said, then it's nothing for you to do but throw away everything and follow Him, and if He didn't, then it's nothing for you to do but enjoy the few minutes you got left the best way you can—by killing somebody or burning down his house or doing

> some other meanness to him. No pleasure, but meanness," he said, and his voice had become almost a snarl.[9]

Like the author of First John, the Misfit sees quite clearly that Christian claims about God are neither speculative nor disinterested. If what Christians claim to know about God is true, then the appropriate response is an act of radical trust (or "faith") and a life of love and freedom that witnesses to Jesus' cross, a life in which everything is indeed "thrown off balance," especially in comparison to what Paul refers to as "the wisdom of the world" (1 Corinthians 1:18–25).

Christians believe they experience the meaning of salvation in the love, freedom, and reconciliation set lose in the world by Jesus' ministry, cross, and resurrection. For them, salvation is just as earthly, this-worldly, and specific as is the first-century Jew from Nazareth.

"What Have You to Do with Us, Jesus of Nazareth?"

According to Mark's Gospel (1:24), that is the question a demon asks Jesus immediately before Jesus casts it out of the man it has possessed. The demon asks that question because it (along with the rest of the demonic powers in Mark's Gospel) knows who Jesus is. "Have you come to destroy us? I know who you are, the Holy One of God?" Jesus' opponents and even his family and his disciples may be uncertain who Jesus is (Mark 3:21), but the demons know. And they know that who Jesus is has everything to do with who they are and what will become of them.

Jesus not only reveals God and in so doing heals and saves; third, he also shapes the lives and identities of those who follow him. In the process of following Jesus, Christians come to understand who he is, and they experience something that they describe as being conformed to him; they claim that Christ is living in them and they are living in him. What Christians know about Jesus demands an act of faith and offers the hope of new life. They find themselves called to a particular form of life that they refer to as "discipleship." To know Jesus as the human face of God and to encounter God's grace and love in him is to be called to a particular way of being in the world. Christian discipleship, life lived in response to Jesus of Nazareth, has a definite form or shape about it, which it receives from him. It is a way of living shaped by his life, death, and resurrection. In the New Testament, Christians find it impossible to describe their faith, who they are, and what they understand themselves to be about in the world apart from him

Three implications of the relation between Jesus and the life of discipleship are especially important for understanding Christian identity. In the first place, the love and freedom of God that Christians see in Jesus frees them from a self-centered existence, which manifests itself in pride and selfishness, and reminds them that to live truly is to live in dependence on God's grace. One of the most powerful statements of this conviction is John Calvin's interpretation of Paul's claim in 1 Corinthians 6:19–20: "You are not your own; . . . you were bought with a price." Calvin writes:

> We are not our own: let not our reason nor our will, therefore, sway our plans and deeds. We are not our own: let us therefore not set it as our goal to seek what is expedient for us according to the flesh. . . . Conversely, we are God's: let us therefore live for him and die for him. We are God's: let his wisdom and will therefore rule all our actions. We are God's: let all the parts of our life accordingly strive toward him as our only lawful goal.[10]

Second, to be a disciple of Jesus is to have one's life turned around and transformed. Christians call this experience "conversion," and it can assume a variety of forms. It can refer to specific, dramatic moments, such as that moment in the parable of the Prodigal Son (Luke 15:11–32) when the son "came to himself" and returned from the far country to his father's home. Or it can refer to the transformation that takes place over the course of a lifetime whereby God's grace overcomes an individual's self-centeredness and frees that person to live in obedience to Jesus of Nazareth.

Christian faith is not simply something that people add to their dossiers, like a list of schools attended or jobs held. The New Testament describes the decision to trust the God revealed in Jesus of Nazareth as an act that makes a decisive claim on people's lives and leads them in a different direction and down a different path than they were previously traveling. It is a "turning around." Mark's Gospel, for example, tells the story of a rich man who asked Jesus what he had to do to inherit eternal life (Mark 10:17–22). He had observed the commandments since his youth. But when Jesus tells him to do one final thing—"Go, sell what you own, and give the money to the poor, and you will have treasure in heaven; then come, follow me"—the rich man goes away in sorrow, "for he had great possessions." The point of Mark's story is not that Christians must sell all their possessions, but that Christian discipleship is not simply one more in a list of credits and accomplishments on one's curriculum vitae, like membership in a local civic club or political party. It is a commitment that leads one in a new direction and can be pursued only by means of God's grace and by a determined single-mindedness.

Third, Christian identity is profoundly relational. Christians believe that all of human life is lived before God and that they can live that way because they have been baptized into the life, death, and resurrection of Jesus Christ. Furthermore, in their baptisms into Christ's body, they live before God in the company of their neighbors. It is here—in Christ and before God—that Christians have their true and lasting identity. For the apostle Paul, true self-knowledge comes only at the end of time, on "that day," when people will be face-to-face with God: "For now we see in a mirror, dimly, but then we will see face to face. Now I know only in part; then I shall know fully, even as I have been fully known" (1 Corinthians 13:12.) At the end of the fourth century, Augustine of Hippo used this text from Paul to begin his reflections on the nature of memory in his *Confessions*: "Let me know you, for you are the God who knows me; *let me recognize you as you have recognized me*."[11] For Christians, the face of God is the face of Jesus. But here there is also an important tension in Christian identity. On the one hand, Christians claim that their true identity is to be found in their life before God. On the other hand, they also claim that we do not truly know God unless we know how God is disposed toward us. In other words, Christian identity has two equally important dimensions. We know the truth about ourselves only when we understand ourselves in relation to God. And we understand who God truly is only when we know God as our creator and redeemer. These two sides to Christian identity—who we are in relation to God, and who God is in relation to us—are intelligible in Christian faith only in the one person, Jesus of Nazareth, who alone is both truly and authentically human and at the same time "God with us" (Matthew 1:23).

Perhaps the closest human analogy to this Christian claim is what some people experience in a marriage or an especially close friendship. In my relationship to my spouse and friends, I may discover truths about myself that were previously hidden from me. In the extended experience of loving and being loved, I may discover things about myself, both good and bad, which come to light only in the depth of those relationships. We come to a deeper knowledge of who we are only in our relationships to others. And Christians believe that the deepest truths about themselves are disclosed in their encounter with and relationship to Jesus Christ.

Apart from Jesus, therefore, Christian faith has no center, shape, or focus. Jesus is the light in the prism of faith that enables Christians to know God, to understand the meaning of salvation, and finally to know the truth about themselves. Jesus Christ is nothing less than the spectacles through which people of faith understand the truth about themselves and their world.

What Does Jesus Have to Do with the Church?

We began by asking whether there could ever be a Church Without Christ. Not only is Jesus the mirror in which Christians understand who they truly are, but he also gives the church its identity. The two are, of course, inseparable. Because they are "baptized into Christ," Christians have their identity in him—in his body—and one dimension of Christ's body is the church

(1 Corinthians 12:13; Galatians 3:27). Hence, though there is no Christian identity apart from Christ, so too there is no Christian identity apart from the church. And the identity of the church, like that of individual Christians, is shaped by the figure of Jesus.

Christian identity is formed when life is lived in the context of the church, the body of Christ and the people of God. But Christians have long realized that they must be careful about the relation between Jesus and the church. The church does not exist as an end in itself. It exists for only one reason: to witness to God's reconciling work in Jesus. Whenever the existence of the church becomes more important than the task it is called to perform, then the meaning and practice of Christian faith become distorted. Through the last third of the twentieth century, the membership numbers of many Protestant denominations have sharply declined. The ongoing temptation for those denominations is to become preoccupied with survival, to make numbers—either members or money—the primary focus. To do so, however, is to neglect their true calling. When Jesus said, "For those who want to save their life will lose it, and those who lose their life for my sake, and for the sake of the gospel, will save it" (Mark 8:35), he was speaking not only to those around him but to his disciples today as well.

The church does not define who Jesus is; rather, Jesus defines who the church is and what it is called to be and do. This conviction was an important part of the Theological Declaration of Barmen, written in 1934 by a Confessional Synod of the German Evangelical Church. Confronted by the stark reality of Hitler's Third Reich and its demand that Christians in Germany pledge their loyalty to the government, some Christians felt called by God to state unequivocally that Jesus Christ alone is Lord of the church:

> The Christian Church is the congregation of the brethren in which Jesus Christ acts presently as the Lord in Word and sacrament through the Holy Spirit. As the church of pardoned sinners, it has to testify in the midst of a sinful world, with its message as with its order, that it is solely

> his property, and that it lives and wants to live solely from his comfort and from his direction in the expectation of his appearance.[12]

Jesus gives direction and therein identity to Christian churches. In the words of John's Gospel, Jesus is "the way, and the truth, and the life" (John 14:6): Jesus shows churches who they are called to be and what they should be about in the world.

The Second Vatican Council in the early 1960s emphasized the importance of the meaning and purpose of the church. From Vatican II, Christians have learned that it is not possible to understand what the church is and what it should be doing in the world without first knowing the identity of the one it believes to be Lord of the church and Lord of the world. After Vatican II, in the language of Christian theology, Christians came to the conclusion that questions about "ecclesiology" (the doctrine of the church) could not be resolved without first addressing questions about "Christology" (the doctrine of the person and work of Jesus Christ). Both Christian individuals and communities find their true identity in Jesus Christ. This theological conviction matters because in every generation the church is tempted to forget who has called it into existence and whom it is called to serve. The claim that Jesus is the Lord of all things gives the church a theological principle by which to measure its faithfulness. The issue of faithfulness is just as important to the church as it was to ancient Israel. One of the great fears of the writers of the Old Testament, especially the authors of Deuteronomy, was that Israel would forget the God who brought it out of bondage in Egypt and led it into a land flowing with milk and honey, and that when life became comfortable, Israel would turn to other gods and no longer worship Yahweh. In order to avoid this fate, the writers of Deuteronomy repeatedly urge Israel to remember its history with God. Similarly, the apostle Paul urges the Christians at Corinth to celebrate the Lord's Supper by remembering the story that is its setting:

> For I received from the Lord what I also handed on to you, that the Lord Jesus on the night when he was betrayed took

> a loaf of bread, and when he had given thanks, he broke it and said, "This is my body that is [broken] for you. Do this in remembrance of me." (1 Corinthians 11:23–24)

Only insofar as the church finds its identity in Jesus of Nazareth will it be faithful to the good news it is called to confess, proclaim, and live. He gives the church its true identity, sustains and encourages it, and also stands over against it, calling it to faithful discipleship in the world. The church belongs to Jesus and not him to it. That is why Christians sing:

> The church's one foundation is Jesus Christ her Lord;
> She is his new creation by water and the word;
> From heaven he came and sought her to be his holy bride;
> With his own blood he bought her, and for her life he died.
> (Samuel J. Stone)

Christian thinking about faith and life finds itself constantly returning to Jesus of Nazareth in order to find its way in the world. When it no longer looks to its center and to the cross that stands there, Christian faith loses its way and becomes confused. Jesus Christ is the means by which Christians understand a living and dynamic faith, one that occasionally assumes new forms of discipleship. Christian thinking and living begins and ends with Jesus of Nazareth. He matters because he is God's material presence in the world.

Chapter Two

Who Was Jesus, Really?

Christian reflection about Jesus of Nazareth begins with the Bible. Our knowledge of him is for the most part limited to what Scripture tells us. Although there are brief allusions to Jesus in other first-century literature (for example, the Jewish historian Josephus and gospels that are not included in the canon), the New Testament gives us the only substantial picture of the so-called "historical Jesus." When theologians and biblical scholars use that phrase, they usually intend a distinction between the "Jesus of history," the figure from the first third of the first century who was born in Galilee and executed in Jerusalem—and the "Jesus of faith," the Jesus of the creeds and theology of the early church. The distinction often presupposes that the Jesus of history is not necessarily the Jesus in whom the church believes. For example, historians unequivocally affirm that Jesus was Jewish, and yet if you closely examine early Christian creeds, such as the Apostles' Creed or the Nicene Creed, you will find no indication that the Jesus who was "conceived by the Holy Ghost, born of the Virgin Mary," and who "suffered under Pontius Pilate" was Jewish.

When Christians think about Jesus, they begin with Scripture's description of him because it is only there that they have access to the Jesus of history. In Christian history there have been many attempts to discover the "real" or conclusive identity of the Jesus of history. None of these "conclusive" historical portraits, however, has gained widespread approval in the church. Biblical scholars and theologians have eventually shown each of them to be more a reflection of the historian than of the historical figure for whom they are searching. But despite repeated setbacks, the search for the historical Jesus continues and probably always will. Why is that? Frequently in Christian history there have been periods in which Christian faith has had to be revised because of major changes in the historical and cultural context in which the church found itself. That happened during the sixteenth century in Europe, for example, with the emergence of Protestant churches. A similar situation developed at the beginning of the nineteenth century, when churches in Europe faced major challenges raised by the Enlightenment of the seventeenth and eighteenth centuries. And in the early twentieth century, following the horror of the First World War, churches had to rethink the meaning of the gospel. So too in the last third of the twentieth century, as Western societies became more diverse racially and ethnically and as the vitality of Christian faith shifted from Western Europe and North America to other parts of the world—Latin America, Africa, and Asia—the question of Christian identity was raised anew (see chapter 6). In its simplest form, that question "Who was the real Jesus?" is a question about the meaning of the gospel, and whenever the meaning of the gospel becomes uncertain, Christians have tried to answer it by returning to the question of the identity of Jesus. "Who is Jesus of Nazareth?" and "How is Jesus good news?" are questions Christians have asked in order to describe the identity and meaning of Christian faith. Quests for the historical Jesus are prompted not simply by idle curiosity or a perverse desire to destroy Christianity but by a genuine desire to make Christian faith intelligible and relevant to new times and situations.

Does the Bible Tell Us Who Jesus Really Was?

Despite the best intentions of those who have participated in these different searches for the historical Jesus, the results have usually been disappointing. The problem has been that those who have gone searching for Jesus have often asked questions that the Bible does not itself ask or answer. This is not to say that the Bible is uninterested in questions of fact and history. On the contrary, most of the writers of the New Testament insist that the gospel they have received—or that has been "handed over" to them and that they are passing on—refers not just to religious ideas but also to historical events. Jesus "suffered under Pontius Pilate," a particular ruler in first-century Israel. The apostle Paul makes this explicit in his First Letter to the Christians in Corinth:

> For I handed on to you as of first importance what I in turn had received: that Christ died for our sins in accordance with the scriptures, and that he was buried, and that he was raised on the third day in accordance with the scriptures, and that he appeared to Cephas, and then to the twelve. Then he appeared to more than five hundred brothers and sisters at one time, most of whom are still alive, though some have died. Then he appeared to James, then to all the apostles. (1 Corinthians 15:3–7)

But while Christians understand faith to refer to historical events, such as Jesus' crucifixion and resurrection, the writers of the New Testament have a curious relation to these events. Though they understand faith to be based on what God has done in history, they seem far more interested in what those events *mean*, in their significance, than in the facts themselves. In an important sense the writers of the New Testament are not historians. They do not have the professional, academic historian's concern for accuracy. In the television series *Dragnet*, from the 1950s, Joe Friday was a detective and not a professional historian, and his only interest was "just the facts, Ma'am." The writers of the New Testament, however, are preachers and evangelists, not detectives. They seem unconcerned about "just the facts" and with whether their version of a story about Jesus differs from that of others. For example, if we examine the description of the empty tomb in Matthew 28, Mark 16, Luke 24, and John 20, it is quickly apparent that the writers of these texts agree that "God raised Jesus from the dead," but they differ significantly about the "facts" of Jesus' resurrection. They do not agree on which women went to the tomb, who got there first, what they found there, how many angels were at the tomb, and what the women did after they went to the tomb. What matters to them is the good news that God raised Jesus from the dead, not the details of the story.

The writers of the New Testament are not primarily historians—and certainly not "historians" in our contemporary understanding of that discipline. They are "evangelists": people who have good news to proclaim. Their news is not about how many women and which women and in what order went to Jesus' tomb on the first day of the week, but the amazing claim that God raised Jesus from the dead. The truth of their message is not dependent on whether there were one or two angels at the tomb, but the startling assertion that the Jesus who died so grotesquely on the cross is the risen, glorified Christ. The truth about Jesus' resurrection is not like the truth of who was at fault in an automobile accident.

This distinction between gospel faith and historical fact can frustrate contemporary readers of the New Testament who want to know only what really happened. When they pose that question to the Bible, readers are often disappointed because the Bible seems far more interested in whether they have heard the good news about God's vindication of Jesus and whether they have responded to that good news with a decision of faith and a commitment to discipleship. When modern readers ask historical questions about the New Testament, they are asking questions that are secondary to its primary message.

The Gospels are not, strictly speaking, "biographies" in our modern understanding of that term. They are not "lives of Jesus." They omit most of Jesus' life. They tell us virtually nothing about Jesus' adolescence, about his intentions, interests, feelings, and motivations. We learn little from them about Jesus' childhood or his relation to his parents and siblings or his life before his baptism by John. They say little about Jesus' intentions and motives. They are not so much biographies of Jesus as they are proclamation of the good news that he is the Christ, the Messiah, and that in him God has reconciled sinful people to God's self and to one another. It is a mistake, therefore, to read the Gospels the same way we read a biography of Abraham Lincoln or of any other major figure in history or a historical account of the American Civil War. If our primary interest in reading them is to establish the precise chronology of events in Jesus' life or to determine the historical accuracy of the events described in them, we will surely miss the most important thing they are trying to tell us.

Furthermore, neither the Gospels nor the rest of the New Testament were written for the world at large or for posterity. Most of what is in the New Testament was written to interpret the meaning of faith for Christian communities facing specific issues and problems at particular times in history. Although the exact nature of these issues, problems, and communities and the precise dates when these texts were written is not always certain, Jesus has a different look about him in each of the Gospels, and the description of his teaching and ministry varies from one Gospel to the next.

In Mark's Gospel, for example, Jesus appears abruptly in the first chapter to be baptized by John the Baptist, with nothing having been said about his birth or youth. The first words we hear from him are a summary of what he will say throughout his ministry—"The time is fulfilled, and the kingdom of God has come near; repent, and believe in the good news" (1:15). Mark's Jesus carries out his ministry with a sense of urgency. He moves "immediately" from one setting to the next. Everything that he says (especially his parables) and does (especially his exorcisms and his miracles) points to the nearness of God's kingdom. Very soon "the Son of Man" will come "in clouds with great power and glory" (13:26) to gather his elect. Although the demons in Mark clearly know who Jesus is, no one else—neither his family, nor his disciples, nor his opponents—quite does, and the reader is left in some doubt (at least until the final event of the cross) as to Jesus' true identity and what it means to call him the Son of God.

In John's Gospel, Jesus is portrayed differently than in Mark. John's Jesus has little to say about a coming kingdom of God. At the beginning of John's story, the reader is told that in Jesus "the Word became flesh and lived among us, and we have seen his glory, the glory as of a father's only son, full of grace and truth" (1:14). John's Jesus makes numerous declarations about his relation to the Father, statements not found in Mark, Matthew, or Luke: "The Father and I are one" (John 10:30). "Whoever sees me sees him who sent me" (12:45). And "I am the bread of life. Whoever comes to me will never be hungry, and whoever believes in me will never be thirsty" (6:35). In Mark's Gospel, Jesus' final words before he dies are words of despair: "My God, my God, why have you forsaken me?" (15:34). In John's Gospel, Jesus' last words before he dies are words of triumph and exaltation: "It is finished" (19:30).

The differences between Mark's description of Jesus and John's raise several questions. The problem is not just that many of the things that Jesus says and does in Mark (or in Matthew or Luke) appear nowhere in John, and that many of the things that Jesus says and does in John appear nowhere in Mark (or in Matthew or Luke), but also that John's Jesus seems to have a different understanding of himself and his mission than does Mark's Jesus. Is there one Jesus in the New Testament, or are there several? If Mark and John were writing biographies of Jesus, we would have serious questions about the apparent differences in their descriptions of Jesus. But that is not what either of them is doing. They are both interpreting the meaning of the core Christian confession that "Jesus is Lord" for quite different first-century Christian communities facing difficult questions concerning the meaning of faithful discipleship in the larger context of Jewish and Hellenistic cultures and the rule of the Roman Empire. The differences in their descriptions of Jesus have to be understood, at least in part, in terms of the different questions and situations they are addressing in those contexts. Who is Jesus of Nazareth, and who are they as Christians if they have recently been cast out of the synagogue, as was perhaps the situation in John's Gospel? Who is Jesus of Nazareth and who are they as Christians as they take their gospel to the larger Hellenistic, Gentile world around the Mediterranean, as was perhaps the situation in Luke's Gospel and in Luke's "history" of the missionary activity of the early church in Acts? Should the good news about Jesus be preached to all people? And if non-Jews became his followers, what was their status in the church?

Although we cannot overlook the differences in the descriptions of Jesus in the Gospels, there are also some striking similarities between them. One of the most important is that all the Gospels are written from the perspective of Easter faith; that is, all the Gospels are written from "this side" of the event that Christians refer to as the "resurrection" of Jesus Christ. Although individual Gospels may differ in how they tell the Easter story, none of them tell their story dispassionately and disinterestedly. Each is written from the perspective that God raised Jesus from the dead and that means this Jesus is the long-awaited Christ, who forgives their sins and will make God's will in heaven a reality on earth. Because he is the resurrected Christ, they can pray with confidence, "Your kingdom come. Your will be done, on earth as it is in heaven" (Matthew 6:10).

The writers of the New Testament believe that in Jesus of Nazareth, God has done something unique and remarkable that has changed them and their world. Their interpretations of who Jesus is and what he calls them to be and do are decisively shaped by their Easter faith and experiences. Readers today cannot understand the Gospels unless they read them from the perspective of the writers' Easter faith. In a very real sense, that means the Gospels must be read backward. They tell the story of Jesus from beginning to end, but as T. S. Eliot once wrote, "In my beginning is my end." And "In my end is my beginning."[1] The Gospels are written by people who confess—finally, in the end—that "Jesus is Lord," but he has been Lord from the beginning. They make that confession for one reason alone: they believe that God raised Jesus from the dead.

The discovery of the role of Easter faith in the writing of the Gospels is one more reason why they cannot be read as biography or "objective" history. The discovery of the confessional intent of the Gospels has not always been accepted with great enthusiasm by the church. To many people, if Jesus did not say what the Bible reports he said, then the Bible is fictitious and false and Christian faith is a sham. If at some point in his life, Jesus did not say, "I am the way, and the truth, and the life" (John 14:6), as John's Gospel reports, then Jesus is not the way, and the truth, and the life—and that statement is false. Such an interpretation, however, confuses good news with biography, and confession with an objective statement of historical facts. From the perspective of Christian faith, it is true that Jesus is the way, and the truth, and the life, regardless of whether Jesus uttered these words. That claim is a statement of Easter faith about the true identity of Jesus of Nazareth. Whether or not Jesus made that claim about himself neither adds to nor detracts from its veracity. For the writers of the New Testament, God raised Jesus from the dead, and because God raised him, he is Lord and Savior of the world.

Because of the confessional nature of the Gospels, we cannot interrogate them in the same way that an attorney might examine a witness concerning the facts of an automobile accident or the way a professional historian might assess claims made in a biography. That does not mean that no historical questions can be asked of the New Testament. An important feature of Christian faith is that at its center is not an idea or a proposition but a person who lived in the first third of the first century. Questions about Christian faith begin with the historical Jesus and what the Bible says about him. It is precisely because Christian faith begins here—with the Jesus of the New Testament—that Christians cannot avoid the difficult task of historical inquiry.

But though it may be that faith cannot avoid historical questions, that does not necessarily mean that Christian faith depends on what historians conclude. Historical truth, after all, is always an interpretation of what historians think likely happened. Historians deal in probabilities, in what is "likely," and not in certainties. Ask a gathering of American historians who specialize in the Civil War what likely caused the conflict. No one will dispute that there was a Civil War, but what likely caused it continues to be hotly debated. And there is nothing "likely" in what Christians claim about Jesus of Nazareth. It is not likely, for example, that God raised Jesus of Nazareth from the grave. The faith of some Christians might be destroyed by the discovery of a first-century tomb in Jerusalem that has the name of Joseph of Arimathea on it and that contains physical remains. For other Christians, believing with Paul that it was not Jesus' flesh and blood that was raised (1 Corinthians 15:50) but his "spiritual body" (15:44), no such historical discovery would shake their faith.

The New Testament is a confessional message for a preaching church; it is not a biography of Jesus. It may not answer all or even most of the questions we want to ask about the historical Jesus, but it does tell us some very important things about him, things that do matter for our understanding of Christian faith.

Was Jesus Jewish?

If we try to find the historical Jesus amid the Christian faith of the New Testament, a number of probable historical facts emerge. Jesus was born around the beginning of what we now call the "first" century, to parents named Mary and Joseph, in the village of Nazareth in Galilee. He probably spoke Aramaic, the language of the region. We know little, if anything, about Jesus' birth and youth before his baptism by John the Baptist. The stories at the beginning of Matthew and Luke (stories not found in Mark or John) are the confession of the early church that the Jesus whom God raised from the dead was from the "beginning" the chosen one, the Messiah, the Christ.

As we noted above, when properly understood, the Gospels should be read backward because they are written from the perspective of Easter faith. When read this way, the stories of Jesus' birth and infancy are the church's response to the question "Who was this Jesus whom God raised from the dead?" The birth stories are the church's confession that from the beginning—or according to John's Gospel (1:1) and the Letter to the Colossians (1:15) "in the beginning"—Jesus was the embodiment, the presence, of God's love and grace in human history. Christians often misunderstand the "miracle" of Jesus' birth, just as they often misunderstand the description of creation in the first two chapters of Genesis. Neither text has anything to do with science. Neither the account of God's creation of all that is nor the stories of Jesus' birth have anything to do with biology. They are about something far more important: God and what God has done. That is, they are theological stories, not scientific accounts. The miracle of Jesus' birth has nothing to do with the biology of his conception, with whether his birth was an example of parthenogenesis or was a "virgin birth." The miracle celebrated in the Christmas stories is that the man Jesus was like all other human beings born of a woman, but was utterly unlike all other human beings in that he was from the beginning (even from all eternity) the reality of God's love and grace "made flesh" (John 1:14 KJV). Or as Matthew puts it in his story, this Jesus is Emmanuel, which means "God is with us" (Matthew 1:23).

The opening chapters of Matthew and Luke do point to one historical fact that is of great importance for understanding who Jesus is. The New Testament leaves no doubt that Jesus is Jewish. The first chapter of Matthew (1:1–16) traces Jesus' genealogy from Abraham through David to Joseph and Mary. The third chapter of Luke (3:23–38) traces Jesus' lineage from Joseph back to Adam. These two genealogies differ in fascinating ways, but they agree on one important matter. Jesus cannot be known properly apart from the history and faith of Israel. Christians believe that all the promises of God to Israel come to fruition in him, but at the same time Jesus cannot be understood apart from God's ongoing covenantal history with Israel. In Matthew's Gospel, Jesus is the "God's Son" (27:54), but from the beginning he is also "the son of David" (1:1). Jesus, therefore, is unintelligible apart from the faith and history of Israel, which is also to say he is unintelligible apart from his own faith and history. Jesus was neither Catholic nor Protestant: he was Jewish. The church has insisted that the Old and New Testaments make up one "canon" or one Bible because it has long recognized that without the Old Testament or Hebrew Scriptures, it would not be able to understand what is in the New Testament or its most basic confession: Jesus is the Messiah, the anointed one of God, the Christ.

Unfortunately Christians have not always acknowledged that Jesus is Jewish nor appreciated the significance of that historical fact for Christian faith. In the early church there were attempts to expunge the Old Testament and all references to Israel from the Bible. Someone unfamiliar with Christian faith could read the Apostles' Creed and the Nicene Creed and find no suggestion that Jesus was Jewish. In the *Book of Confessions* of the Presbyterian Church (U.S.A), it is not until The Confession of 1967, a document written in the aftermath of the Holocaust, that Jesus is recognized unequivocally as "a Palestinian Jew."[2] The National Socialist Party (Nazis) in Germany during the 1930s denied that Jesus was Jewish and insisted that he was Aryan. The attempt to deny that Jesus is Jewish has a long, sordid, and tragic history not only in Western culture and history, but also within the church. The Bible, however, makes it difficult to do that. One has to shut one's eyes to most of what is in Scripture not to recognize its affirmation that Jesus is a child of Israel.

The importance of the unity of the Old and New Testaments is only one reason why it is important to recognize that Jesus was Jewish. Others are equally important. If we are to understand what Jesus says and does in the Gospels, we must read those texts in the context of his Jewish faith and heritage. Christians have many things they want to say about Jesus, but one of those should be (but rarely is) that he was a devout Jew. Jesus worshiped in synagogues, was familiar with Jewish Scripture and quoted it, affirmed God's commandments to Israel, and prayed to Israel's God. Unless the Jesus of the Gospels is understood to be Jewish, much of what the New Testament says about him will be misinterpreted or unintelligible.

The claim that Jesus was a devout Jew does not mean that he agreed with every form of Jewish faith in his time. Just as Protestantism today (not to mention Christianity) is remarkably diverse, so too first-century Judaism was anything but monolithic. The New Testament describes different groups within first-century Israel—Pharisees, scribes, Sadducees, Zealots, Essenes, and rulers of the temple—who disagree among themselves about how to understand their faith. The Gospels describe ongoing controversies between Jesus and some of these groups, especially the Pharisees. A central point in these disagreements is the interpretation of Jewish law. On the one hand, pious Jew that he is, Jesus affirms the importance and abiding validity of the law:

> Do not think that I have come to abolish the law or the prophets; I have come not to abolish but to fulfill. For truly I tell you, until heaven and earth pass away, not one letter, not one stroke of a letter, will pass from the law until all is accomplished. (Matthew 5:17–18)

In response to a scribe's question about which is the most important of the commandments (Mark 12:28–31), Jesus quotes Deuteronomy 6:4–5 and Leviticus 19:18. One should love God with all of one's heart, soul, and strength and one's neighbor as oneself. In numerous other contexts, Jesus affirms the validity of Jewish law. Yet he also demonstrates a remarkable freedom in relation to the law. In a variety of situations, Jesus insists that the law is not an end in itself but must be understood in the larger context of obedience to God's love and grace. When confronted by the Pharisees with a woman caught in adultery, who according to Jewish law should be stoned, Jesus responds, "Let anyone among you who is without sin be the first to throw a stone at her" (John 8:7). When Jesus enters a synagogue on the Sabbath and encounters a man with a withered hand, he does not hesitate to heal him, even in the presence of the Pharisees and even though such an act violates laws governing the observance of the Sabbath. Jesus asks the Pharisees, "Is it lawful to do good or to do harm on the sabbath, to save life or to kill?" (Mark 3:4).

An indication of the way in which Jesus both affirms and yet transcends Jewish law is his remarkable exercise of authority. Israel had known many prophets who came with the word of the Lord on their lips. The prophets of the Old Testament often prefaced what they had to say to the people of Israel with the words "Thus says the Lord" (as in Isaiah 29:22). Jesus, however, does not begin his teaching and preaching with these familiar words. Furthermore, he dares to claim the authority to interpret the law. In the Sermon on the Mount in Matthew 5–7, Jesus says, "You have heard that it was said to those of ancient times" (5:21), and then quotes the commandments concerning murder, adultery, divorce, lying, vengeance, and treatment of the neighbor. Jesus rehearses these familiar commandments and says, "You have heard that it was said, 'An eye for an eye and a tooth for a tooth.' But I say to you, Do not resist an evildoer" (5:38–39).

Jesus does not deny the validity of the law. It was, after all, given by God, and what God gives is good. But he does insist that the law must be understood and practiced in the broader context of God's love and grace. What Jesus has to say about the law is authoritative because he says it: "But I say to you. . . ." His authority to interpret the law, to put it in its proper context, has something to do with who he is and what he does, something to do with his relation to the one he calls "Father."

The New Testament makes it very clear that Jesus is not merely one of Israel's prophets. That point is demonstrated by how Jesus speaks to God in the Gospels. In Mark's description of Jesus in the Garden of Gethsemane on the night of his arrest, Jesus prays: "Abba, Father, for you all things are possible; remove this cup from me; yet not what I want, but what you want" (14:36). The use of "Abba" to refer to God suggests a relationship of remarkable intimacy, affectionate language a child might use in addressing a parent. Not only does Jesus dare to speak to Holy God in such intimate language, but he also teaches his disciples to do so as well. The prayer that Jesus teaches his disciples and that they continue to pray to this day begins, "Father, hallowed be your name" (Luke 11:2). The New Testament scholar Eduard Schweizer sums up the implication of Jesus' use of the term "Abba" or "Father": "What is new is not that Jesus taught men to call God 'Father'; it is that a people more sensitive than any other to the distance between God and man, between God and the world, were granted the freedom to say 'Abba.'"[3] Jesus' freedom in his relation to the law of God and in his use of the term "Abba" to address God demonstrates a remarkable authority in what he says and does, an authority that was offensive to many people in the first century and is no less so to some today.

How Does the New Testament Identify Jesus?

The New Testament identifies Jesus in a number of ways. First and perhaps most important, it tells stories about him. The

Gospels are collections of stories about Jesus—some that claim to be told by him and others that are about him. Each Gospel is itself a larger story about Jesus. Mark assembles numerous stories about Jesus and out of those stories constructs his own interpretation—a larger story or Gospel—about the identity and significance of Jesus. In addition to stories, the New Testament also includes letters, many written by the apostle Paul, and these letters often describe Jesus' identity and his significance. Stories and letters are not the only literary genre in the New Testament. It also includes hymns and creeds that make important statements about Jesus. Hence the Bible identifies Jesus in various ways by means of a variety of literary genres.

Yet another way it does so is by means of what are sometimes described as "titles." Jesus is given many different titles in the New Testament, and each title provides him a form of identity. Some of the most frequent and important are "the Christ" (*Christos*) or Messiah, Lord (*kyrios*), Son of God, Son of Man, Son of David, Rabbi or Teacher, High Priest, Savior, and King of the Jews. Each makes a distinctive claim about who he is, and each must be understood in the historical context of Jewish and Hellenistic thought during the first century.

Two basic points are important about these titles. The first concerns the difficult question Did Jesus use any of these titles to refer to himself? And if he did so, what did he mean by them? Did Jesus refer to himself as the Christ/Messiah or as the Son of God, and did he mean by them what the post-Easter church meant when it used them to say who Jesus was and is? This is yet another example of an important historical question that we cannot answer with certainty only on the basis of the evidence in the New Testament. The best New Testament scholarship suggests it is unlikely that Jesus referred to himself as either the Messiah or the Son of God. These are titles that the Easter church, living on this side of the resurrection, attributed to Jesus in order to confess its faith in him. The writers of the Gospels put these titles into Jesus' mouth in order to make it clear who they believed him to be. As far as the early, post-Easter church was concerned, Jesus was indeed the Messiah and the Son of God from "the beginning" (John 1:1), regardless of whether he made such a claim for himself or not. The church's faith that the one whom Jesus called "Abba" had indeed raised him from the dead—that faith enabled the church to identify Jesus as Messiah and Son of God.

Part of the problem, as we noted previously, is that the New Testament does not give us reliable historical material for determining what Jesus thought about himself. Nor does the New Testament give us the necessary evidence to determine whether Jesus actually used the titles that the writers of the New Testament attributed to him, and if he did, what he meant by them. The title "Son of Man" is a case in point. It was not a title invented either by Jesus or the early church. It is a term from the literature of Jewish apocalyptic (writings that look forward to the final triumph of God over all things, including evil, and the restoration of Israel to its place of prominence among the nations of the world). For example, Daniel 7:13–14 refers to that agent of God who will end the present age and inaugurate a new heaven and a new earth:

> As I watched in the night visions, I saw one like a human being [or, son of man] coming with the clouds of heaven. And he came to the Ancient One and was presented before him. To him was given dominion and glory and kingship, that all peoples, nations, and languages should serve him. His dominion is an everlasting dominion that shall not pass away, and his kingdom is one that shall never be destroyed.

In the Gospels, Jesus occasionally uses the term "Son of Man" to refer to himself, as in Matthew 8:20: "Foxes have holes, and the birds of the air have nests; but the Son of Man has nowhere to lay his head." In other texts, however, Jesus appears to refer to a Son of Man who is not to be identified with himself, as in Luke 12:8–10: "And I tell you, everyone who acknowledges me before others, the Son of Man also will acknowledge before the angels of God." If the texts that speak of the Son of Man in the future tense are more likely authentic words of Jesus than those in the present tense, then it seems likely that while the church used the title "Son of Man" to proclaim who it believed Jesus to be, it is unlikely that Jesus used the title in reference to himself.

There is no historical evidence that Abraham Lincoln ever referred to himself as the Great Emancipator. And yet during his lifetime, and especially in the years immediately following his death, that became a primary title by which Lincoln was known. Lincoln was indeed the Great Emancipator, even if he never referred to himself by that title.

A second consideration concerns the meaning of the titles given to Christ. The church did not simply take familiar titles from its Jewish tradition, such as Messiah and Suffering Servant, apply them to Jesus, and in so doing give him a new identity. The relation between Jesus and the titles the post-Easter church uses to identify him is more complex than that. Most of the titles had familiar meanings for first-century Jews and Greeks, but the writers of the New Testament do not simply apply those original, well-known meanings to Jesus. In practically every case they give them a new meaning in light of what the Gospels report about Jesus. The titles do not entirely lose their original meaning, but they are reinterpreted in the context of the stories the Gospels tell, and those reinterpretations are of major significance.

For example, the Gospel of Mark is especially concerned with what it means to say that Jesus is the "Son of God." Before Jesus' death in chapter 15, no figure in Mark's Gospel is allowed to refer to Jesus as Son of God and go unrebuked except the demons. Only the demons know Jesus' true identity and understand what it means to call him Son of God. "Whenever the unclean spirits saw him, they fell down before him and shouted, 'You are the Son of God!' But he sternly ordered them not to make him known" (3:11–12).

Neither Jesus' disciples nor his family recognize who he truly is. The most obvious example of this "blindness" is Peter's response to Jesus at Caesarea Philippi in Mark 8:27–33, a story that immediately follows Jesus' healing of a blind man at Bethsaida (8:22–26). After asking the disciples (and those of us reading this text), "Who do people say that I am?" Jesus next asks them, "But who do you say that I am?" Peter apparently answers correctly, "You are the Messiah [or, the Christ]." Jesus then proceeds to tell the disciples what awaits him in Jerusalem as the Messiah. "Then he began to teach them that the Son of Man must undergo great suffering, and be rejected by the elders, the chief priests, and the scribes, and be killed, and after three days rise again" (8:31). Furthermore, Mark adds, "He said all this quite openly" (8:32a). Peter responds with words that suggest his shock, horror, and dismay: "And Peter took him aside and began to rebuke him" (8:32b). Clearly what Peter means by the title "Messiah" or "Christ" is not what Jesus is talking about. What kind of Messiah is Peter looking for? Mark does not tell us, but it certainly is not a crucified Messiah. The incident closes with chilling words from Jesus. "Get behind me, Satan! For you are setting your mind not on divine things but on human things" (8:33). The translation by the Revised Standard Version (RSV) is better: "For you are not on the side of God, but of men." This is a pivotal event in Mark's story about Jesus. A line is drawn in the sand as to Jesus' identity, and the remainder of the narrative rushes to its conclusion in Jerusalem.

In Mark's Gospel the only person permitted to call Jesus the Son of God and go unrebuked is someone who does not follow him from Nazareth to Jerusalem and would seem to know little or nothing about him. From Mark's perspective, however, this person knows the only thing necessary to understand what kind of Messiah Jesus is. That figure is the Roman Centurion who, according to Mark, stands facing the crucified Jesus and says, "Truly this man was God's Son!" (Mark 15:39). (Once again I prefer the translation of the RSV: "Truly this man was the Son of God.") The centurion understands who Jesus is as Son of God because he stands facing Jesus on the cross. Mark's point is obvious. Jesus is not simply Israel's long-expected Messiah. He is the crucified Messiah and the crucified Son of God.

The titles that the New Testament uses to identify Jesus, including Christ/Messiah and Son of God, are reinterpreted in the Gospel narratives. The same is also true of what appears in the hymns (such as Philippians 2:5–11 and Colossians 1:15–20) and creeds (such as 1 Corinthians 15:3–7 and Romans 1:3–4) used in the New Testament to identify Jesus as the Christ. Each must be interpreted in light of the Jesus stories that we have in the four Gospels. In order to know how the writers of the New Testament understood these titles and what they were trying to say about Jesus' identity, it is important to understand what the titles meant in their original Jewish or Greek context. At the same time, each of them is reinterpreted by the stories the Gospels tell about Jesus. And what is true of these New Testament titles is also true of the other claims it makes about Jesus. They too must be understood in relation to the stories the New Testament tells.

Who Is Jesus in the Stories of the Gospels?

Because the New Testament is an "evangelical" text—written to confess and proclaim that Jesus is the Christ, the world's Savior—it is not a "historical" text in the way we commonly understand that term. It is not primarily concerned with chronology and factual accuracy. It is telling a "historical" story in that it is describing Jesus of Nazareth, a first-century Jew who lived in Galilee. What it has to say about Jesus, however, goes far beyond what any historian can verify. Because of this confessional nature of the New Testament, we do not know what Jesus thought about himself or whether he understood himself to be the Christ and the Messiah. We do know that after his baptism by John the Baptist, Jesus conducted a brief ministry first in Galilee and then in Jerusalem. In his ministry Jesus taught primarily by means of parables, and most of them had a single theme: the coming kingdom of God. A single verse in the first chapter of Mark's Gospel summarizes the content of Jesus' teaching, preaching, and healing ministry: "The time is fulfilled, and the kingdom of God has come near; repent, and believe in the good news" (1:15). At the center of Jesus' teaching, preaching, and healing is the symbol of the kingdom of God, and Jesus' parables and his healing and exorcisms communicate something of this kingdom's presence and power.

Jesus' message does not focus primarily on a new form of morality or a new style of politics. Nor does Jesus seem interested in teaching new religious beliefs. One reality dominates what he says and does: repentance in preparation for the coming of God's kingdom. If you read through the Gospels, the centrality of the kingdom of God in what Jesus says and does is obvious—so obvious that it is difficult to understand how so many of those who have searched the New Testament for the real Jesus, the Jesus of the first century, could have missed it. And yet many of the portraits of Jesus that have emerged in the nineteenth and twentieth centuries describe a teacher of morality, or a great psychologist, or a spiritual leader, or a community organizer, or a political revolutionary. These interpretations of Jesus have little to do with the Jesus described in the Gospels. The gospel that Jesus preaches does indeed have significant implications for morality, psychological health, spiritual peace, life together, and politics, but only if they are understood to be implications of Jesus' primary emphasis on the nearness of God's kingdom.

Four features of Jesus' teaching, preaching, and healing are important for understanding his identity. In the first place, it is significant that Jesus describes the coming kingdom of God by means of parables. Jesus does not say. "The kingdom of God is this," or "the kingdom of God is that." He says, "The kingdom of God is *like*," and then tells a parable such as this one:

> With what can we compare the kingdom of God, or what parable will we use for it? It is like a mustard seed, which, when sown upon the ground, is the smallest of all the seeds on earth; yet when it is sown it grows up and becomes the greatest of all shrubs, and puts forth branches, so that the birds of the air can make nests in its shade. (Mark 4:30–32)

Why did Jesus teach in parables? That question cannot be answered conclusively, but given the content of Jesus' parables, it seems likely that the nature of the kingdom (and therein the identity of the one who tells parables about it) is such that it cannot be described in objective, factual terms. The kingdom of God is what is ultimately and finally real, but it is hidden in what the world mistakenly believes to be ultimately and finally real. Jesus intends his parables to evoke from his audience a response of repentance, conversion, and transformation. Because the parables are a form of metaphor, they enable those who hear them to identify with the familiar world in which the parables are set and to be drawn into them. But when people enter the parables' familiar, ordinary world, they also encounter the hidden and the extraordinary and may be unexpectedly transformed.

Second, Jesus' parables turn the familiar, ordinary world upside down. What is considered reality in the familiar world is transformed in God's kingdom. In the familiar world one gets what one deserves. In God's kingdom, however, the miracle of God's grace replaces the "just deserts" of what one deserves. In Jesus' parable of the laborers in the vineyard in Matthew 20:1–16, all the workers are paid the same wage, regardless of how long they have worked. Those who have worked all day are paid the same as those who were hired at the last minute. Even worse, those who worked all day are forced to wait, while those who came late are paid first. When those hired at the beginning of the day see that they are not being paid more than those who worked only a few minutes, they grumble about the obvious unfairness and injustice. The owner of the vineyard replies, "Am I not allowed to do what I choose with what belongs to me? Or are you envious because I am generous?" (20:15) And then Jesus concludes, "So the last will be first, and the first will be last."

The kingdom of God, to which Jesus calls those who would be his disciples, turns the commonly accepted values of the world upside down. At one place in Mark's Gospel, Jesus makes this explicit without using a parable:

> If any want to become my followers, let them deny themselves and take up their cross and follow me. For those who want to save their life will lose it, and those who lose their life for my sake, and for the sake of the gospel, will save it. (8:34–35)

God's coming kingdom and the discipleship to which Jesus calls his disciples are characterized by the reign of God's grace, by self-denial on the part of those who participate in the kingdom, and by the reversal of what is normally considered gaining and losing, life and death.

Third, in several texts in the Gospels, Jesus seems to understand the coming kingdom of God to be closely tied to his ministry and perhaps to his person. Some of these texts suggest that a decision for or against Jesus is also a decision for or against the kingdom of God. In his instructions to his twelve disciples, Jesus says, "You will be hated by all because of my name" (Matthew 10:22). And when the disciples of John the Baptist ask Jesus whether he is the long-awaited Messiah, the one who is to come, he tells them to report to John what they have seen and heard: "The blind receive their sight, the lame walk, . . . the poor have good news brought to them" (Luke 7:22). And he adds, "And blessed is anyone who takes no offense at me" (7:23). In what Jesus says and does, there is indeed evidence that he believes the kingdom of God is erupting with great power and glory in the mustard seed that is his ministry.

Not only does Jesus teach the kingdom of God by means of parables; the Gospels, written from the perspective of the church's Easter faith, suggest that Jesus himself is *the* parable of God's kingdom of love and grace. It is important that the Gospels are not just a series of parables or sayings about Jesus. Jesus' parables of the kingdom appear in the framework of larger Gospel narratives about Jesus' teaching and ministry, and without this larger framework, Jesus' parables would be open to misrepresentation. What Jesus says in his parables must be understood in relation to the Gospels' description of what Jesus does. The one clarifies the other. What Jesus does—his ministry, healing, and exorcisms—must be understood in light of the parables he tells. Not only does Jesus teach about God's kingdom of love and grace; he also enacts the reality of that kingdom in his own life and ministry. Not only does Jesus teach that the first shall be last and the last first, but also in his ministry he intentionally seeks out those who are on the margins of society—the lepers, the maimed, the tax collectors, the prostitutes—as special recipients of God's love and grace. And through the Gospels he calls his disciples, the church, and the world to do the same. From the perspective of the church's Easter faith, Jesus of Nazareth is *the* parable of God's kingdom. On the one hand he is familiar and ordinary: in the language of the Letter to the Hebrews, he is "one who in every respect has been tested as we are, yet without sin" (4:15). Yet in the midst of his ordinariness, the extraordinary and the miraculous appear.

Fourth, according to the Gospels, Jesus believes that the kingdom of God is either appearing in the world in the midst of his ministry or at least is a reality that will appear very soon. Jesus' words and actions suggest that he believes God's kingdom hovers on the horizon of the present moment. In his instruction to his disciples in Matthew 10, Jesus tells them that when they are persecuted, they are to flee to another town, "for truly I tell you, you will not have gone through all the towns of Israel before the Son of Man comes" (10:23). And in Mark's Gospel, Jesus tells the disciples, "There are some standing here who will not taste death until they see that the kingdom of God has come with power" (9:1).

Jesus' claims concerning the nearness of the kingdom posed serious difficulties for the early church. There is some evidence in the New Testament that early Christian communities, those formed soon after the Easter appearances of the risen Christ, expected the kingdom to come very soon—indeed, before some of them would "taste death"—and after the resurrection they associated the coming of the kingdom with the return of Jesus. "Then comes the end, when he [Christ] hands over the kingdom to God the Father, after he has destroyed every ruler and every authority and power" (1 Corinthians 15:24). In some of his earliest letters, Paul seems to believe that the return of Christ will take place very soon. To the Christians at Thessalonica, Paul writes:

> For the Lord himself, with a cry of command, with the archangel's call and with the sound of God's trumpet, will descend from heaven, and the dead in Christ will rise first. Then we who are alive, who are left, will be caught up in the clouds together with them to meet the Lord in the air; and so we will be with the Lord forever. (1 Thessalonians 4:16–17)

A major problem for the faith of the early church was the fact that Jesus did not return "very soon," at least not in the way Paul and others expected. The church dealt with that difficult issue in various ways. Often it simply ignored Jesus' teaching that the kingdom is coming soon. In so doing it had to reinterpret the meaning of Christian hope as is given in the penultimate verse of the New Testament: "The one who testifies to these things says, 'Surely I am coming soon.' Amen. Come, Lord Jesus!" (Revelation 22:20).

Yet another approach has been to spiritualize and privatize Jesus' message and insist that the kingdom he proclaims and enacts is simply an inner peace of the soul. Such interpretations appeal mistakenly to texts like Luke 17:20–21:

> Once Jesus was asked by the Pharisees when the kingdom of God was coming, and he answered, "The kingdom of God is not coming with things that can be observed; nor will they say, 'Look, here it is!' or 'There it is!' For, in fact the kingdom of God is among you."

The problem with this "spiritual" interpretation is that it simply does not cohere with the rest of Jesus' teaching about the kingdom of God. In Luke's Gospel, Jesus begins his ministry in his hometown of Nazareth by going to the synagogue and reading from Isaiah. "The Spirit of the Lord is upon me, because he has anointed me to bring good news to the poor" (Luke 4:18). Jesus' gospel or "good news" is not about how to have a private religious experience, but about "release to the captives," the recovery of vision for the blind, and the freeing of the oppressed. Unlike Isaiah, Jesus not only proclaims this good news, but to their great consternation he also tells his audience, "Today this scripture has been fulfilled in your hearing" (Luke 4:21). The kingdom of God has drawn very near not only because Jesus proclaims this message, but also because in his ministry—for those with eyes to see and ears to hear—he enacts what he proclaims. He sets free those possessed by demons, he heals the blind, and he frees those oppressed by guilt, sin, and the burden of possessions. What the Gospels report as the teaching of Jesus and the meaning of

Christian hope has to do with more than just the soul and more than just individual well-being.

It was perhaps Jesus' sense of the nearness, the imminence, of the kingdom that led him to take his teaching and ministry to Jerusalem. Whatever Jesus' motives were, this decision was fatal. The journey to Jerusalem led him into conflict with both the authorities in the temple, who were charged by the Romans with maintaining public order and peace, and finally the Romans themselves. Jesus was arrested, tried by the Jewish authorities, and then turned over to the Romans, who beat and executed him. The "passion" of Jesus—the events surrounding his trial and execution—receives considerable attention in the Gospels. Indeed, the "plot" of the Gospels builds in intensity the closer Jesus comes to Jerusalem and to crucifixion.

That Jesus of Nazareth was executed by crucifixion is perhaps the most reliable historical fact in the Gospels. But while his death on a cross may be indisputable, the accounts of his arrest, trial, and execution do not answer many historical questions. It is unclear, for example, precisely what the charges against Jesus were. There is some evidence (Mark 14:64 and Matthew 26:65) that Jesus was charged with blasphemy. However, when Jesus is executed by the Romans, all four Gospels in the New Testament report that a sign declaring his crime was affixed to the cross. "The inscription of the charge against him read, 'The king of the Jews'" (Mark 15:26). So what precisely was Jesus' "crime"? New Testament scholars cannot agree. Some argue that Jesus was charged with threatening to destroy the temple and build another (Mark 14:58) or that he committed blasphemy by claiming to be the Messiah (Mark 14:61–64). Others contend that the Jewish leaders of the temple turned Jesus over to the Romans, not because of any religious or theological transgression, but because he had stirred up the large crowds gathered in Jerusalem for Passover, and his preaching about the coming kingdom of God threatened to ignite smoldering Jewish resentment against Roman occupation. It may not have mattered to the Romans whether Jesus was a blasphemer, but his announcement that the kingdom of God was near would have been something else altogether. That message may have sounded like a direct threat to Roman power and rule.

Did the Romans misunderstand Jesus? Nowhere in the Gospels does Jesus announce a political or social program for reorganizing Israel. Jesus was not a political revolutionary, but an apocalyptic prophet, much like John, who preceded him and baptized him, and Paul, who followed him. Jesus was certainly not the first apocalyptic prophet in Israel, but he did differ decisively from all the others—both those who preceded and those who followed him. Jesus proclaimed the reign of God, the triumph of God's will over all things, the coming of God's kingdom, which had drawn very near in his ministry of preaching and healing. After God raised him from the dead, his followers realized that not only had Jesus proclaimed God's kingdom, but also that he himself was the kingdom he had proclaimed. In this Jesus "are hidden all the treasures of wisdom and knowledge" (Colossians 2:3).

In the New Testament, Jesus' death is not finally about Jewish fear of social disorder or Roman misunderstanding of what Jesus was about. Just as in his ministry he forgave sins, so too the meaning of his death has to do with the forgiveness of sin and the re-creation of human beings along with the rest of creation. At the beginning of this chapter we noted that in 1 Corinthians 15:3–5 Paul quotes from an early Christian creed that he received from other Christians: "For I handed on to you as of first importance what I in turn had received: that Christ died for our sins in accordance with the scriptures." For Paul the significance of the death of Jesus is that it does for sinners, including Paul himself, what they cannot possibly do for themselves. "All have sinned" (Romans 3:23), and the consequence of sin is death: "Death came through sin, and so death spread to all because all have sinned" (5:12). In the last two verses of Romans 7, Paul writes, "Wretched man that I am! Who will rescue me from this body of death?" The good news, however, is that "while we still were sinners Christ died for us" (5:8). The significance of Christ's death, therefore, is that "while we were enemies, we were reconciled to God through the death of his Son" (5:10). And because they have been reconciled to God, Paul argues, Christians also have been reconciled to one another and to the world. Paul summarizes the significance of Jesus' death in his Second Letter to the Christians in Corinth:

> All this is from God, who reconciled us to himself through Christ, and has given us the ministry of reconciliation; that is, in Christ God was reconciling the world to himself, not counting their trespasses against them, and entrusting the message of reconciliation to us. (5:18–19)

Chapter Three

How Is Jesus "Savior"?

In chapter 2 we observed that the New Testament identifies Jesus in multiple ways. The Gospels are stories about Jesus, and within those larger narratives are smaller stories or parables that Jesus tells about the kingdom of God. Both the stories told about Jesus and the stories Jesus tells disclose something of his identity. In addition, there are numerous titles, hymns, and creeds in the New Testament that interpret Jesus' identity. Not only are there multiple literary forms in the New Testament, but also quite different things are said about Jesus. Although there is much on which the Gospels agree in their descriptions of Jesus, there are also significant differences among them. Mark's story about Jesus begins with his baptism by John. Jesus appears to be in a hurry and rushes from one scene to the next. The kingdom that Jesus proclaims has drawn near, and Mark tells his story in light of the cross. Only at the cross does the reader learn what the demons have always known: that the crucified Jesus is God's Son. John's Gospel, on the other hand, begins long before Jesus' baptism. Like Genesis it begins "in the beginning" with the Word—"and the Word was with God, and the Word was God" (1:1)—and this Word was made flesh in Jesus of Nazareth and "lived among us, and we have seen his glory, the glory as of a father's only son, full of grace and truth" (1:14). In Mark and John the reader is given two quite different interpretations of Jesus' identity. What are we to make of these differences? Are the four Gospels, not to mention Paul and the rest of the New Testament, all saying the same thing? Are the differences inconsequential? Should we minimize the differences and simply focus on what they seem to have in common? Through the centuries many theologians have dealt with this problem by writing "harmonies" of the Gospels, which try to reduce them to a single coherent narrative or make one of the four Gospels the primary text for the interpretation of the others. Christians have always been tempted to turn the diversity in the New Testament into a single megastory in order to proclaim a clear, concise, and coherent gospel. The so-called "Christmas pageant" in many congregations is often an example of this harmonization of the Gospels. Such "harmony," however, comes at a high price. Invariably something vitally important is lost when some "voices" in the New Testament are marginalized or silenced altogether simply for the sake of clarity, conciseness, and coherence. For example, it is unusual if a Christmas pageant includes the story of Herod's slaughter of Bethlehem's children in Matthew 2:16–18.

One way to understand these differences is by means of the obvious fact that the New Testament was written by not one but multiple authors in different contexts, addressing different needs. We do not know who Mark, Matthew, Luke, and John were, and although we know something about Paul, we know next to nothing about the identities of the authors of the other texts in the New Testament. Both Luke's Gospel and his history of the early church (the Acts of the Apostles) were written in light of the larger question of whether there should be room among the original Jewish followers of Jesus for Gentiles. John's Gospel appears to have been written for a Christian community that has recently either left or been thrown out of a Jewish synagogue. The description of Jesus in the second and third chapters of the Revelation to John is related to the impending possibility of persecution, even martyrdom, of the seven churches to whom the letter is sent. In the New Testament, the diversity of descriptions of Jesus has something to do with the diverse needs of those for whom it was written.

What Do People Want from Jesus?

We have also recognized, especially in Mark's Gospel, that there is confusion among even Jesus' closest followers as to who he truly is and what his kingdom is about. Peter answers Jesus' question "But who do you say that I am?" (Mark 8:29) correctly by identifying him as the Christ or Messiah. Yet as soon as Jesus explains that to be the Messiah means to go to Jerusalem and be crucified, Peter is horrified and takes Jesus aside in order to rebuke him. Mark does not tell us what Peter was expecting in a Messiah, but apparently it had nothing to do with the ignominy of crucifixion. For what or whom was Peter looking? What kind of Messiah or savior did he expect? Mark does not tell us. Was Peter a first-century Zealot, anxiously awaiting a Messiah who would rally Israel and drive the hated Roman army of occupation into the Mediterranean Sea? Or was Peter looking for a Messiah who would restore the throne of David to preeminence among the nations of the earth? Mark simply leaves that to his readers' imaginations.

Nor is Peter the only figure in Mark's Gospel or in the rest of the New Testament who seems to be looking for a Messiah different from the Jesus whom Mark describes. Two chapters after Peter's encounter with Jesus at Caesarea Philippi, Mark tells the story of a conversation between Jesus and the sons of Zebedee, James and John (10:35–45). They make a request of Jesus: "Grant us to sit, one at your right hand and one at your left, in your glory" (10:37). Jesus tells them that they do not understand what they are asking; he asks whether they are able to drink the cup that he drinks and to be baptized with his baptism. Their answer "We are able" (10:39) indicates that they, like Peter, have no idea what Jesus has been anointed to do by the one he calls "Abba." What kind of Messiah were James and John looking for? Once more Mark does not tell us. When the other disciples hear what James and John have requested, they become angry. Their anger and Jesus' response suggests that perhaps what was at issue was an early struggle among Jesus' followers over who would exercise power in Jesus' kingdom. Perhaps James and John had launched a preemptive strike at positions of power and influence. They failed to understand that Jesus' kingdom would not be one in which rulers and "great ones" exercise power over everyone else. Whatever it was that James and John were looking for must have made it impossible for them to understand Jesus' response. "But it is not so among you; but whoever wishes to become great among you must be your servant, and whoever wishes to be first among you must be slave of all" (10:43–44).

What these and other stories in the New Testament suggest is that many who encounter Jesus already know what they are looking for in a Messiah. They already know what they want their deliverer, God's anointed one, to do for them; like Peter, James, and John the only significant question is whether Jesus will deliver, whether he is indeed the Messiah for whom they yearn. And because they already know what they are looking for, their response to Jesus is often bewilderment and dismay: "Is not this the carpenter's son?" (Matthew 13:55). This Jesus cannot possibly be their long-awaited Messiah. Although the term "Messiah," or "Christ," comes to us from the Old Testament, it was by no means only the Jews who were looking for someone who would mend their torn lives, heal their wounded world, and fulfill their deepest longings and dreams. The same has been true for many throughout human history.

As in the first century, so today some people yearn for a political Messiah who will overturn the status quo, whatever it may be, and usher in a new political order. Those who look for their saviors in politics often do so because they understand politics to be what is ultimately important about human life. Not surprisingly, those looking for a political Messiah already know what kind of political commitments their savior should have: usually a politics remarkably similar to their own. For those looking for a political savior in the United States, Jesus becomes a Messiah who supports either the importance of family values, the right to bear arms, free enterprise, and the American way of life—or a Messiah who lives only on the margins of society, who crosses social boundaries, loves the poor and hates the rich, and seeks to overturn established institutions. Both camps have been remarkably successful in finding evidence that the Jesus of the New Testament is precisely the particular political savior for whom they have been waiting.

Other people search for a savior who is altogether different from a political Messiah. Their hope is not in the political order and the social organization of this world but in a spiritual realm that transcends this veil of tears. They yearn for a spiritual Messiah who will tutor their souls and show them the path to heaven. They know that the deepest longings of the human heart and soul cannot be satisfied in this life and in this broken world; they seek a Messiah who will enlighten their souls and enable them to ascend to that which is truly eternal. Not surprisingly, those looking for a spiritual Messiah believe it is the spiritual world and not this physical, material one that is ultimately real. What truly matters is not so much daily bread as bread for the soul. Those who seek such a Messiah often have the luxury of not having to worry about daily bread for themselves and their family.

And then there are those for whom the ultimate goal of human life is an abundant life that manifests itself in financial and material prosperity. Those who seek a prosperity Messiah come from various communities. Some already have more things than they need, but they either want more or they want to justify what they already have. They seek a prosperity Messiah, not because they simply want enough to meet life's basic needs, but also because they want to be rich beyond their wildest dreams. Their Messiah is the one who says, "I came that they might have life, and have it abundantly" (John 10:10), but they misunderstand what Jesus means by "abundant life." For those who already have enough but want much more, salvation is not about just having enough; they dream of having all they can imagine. And the Bible warns us that the imagination is fertile ground for the seeds of idolatry.

What is "salvation" in the New Testament? And what does it mean to call Jesus "Savior"? Given the various, diverse ways the New Testament describes Jesus, it should not be surprising that it also offers multiple descriptions of salvation. One significant interpretation of salvation is that it is the forgiveness of sins. Because of what they read in the New Testament, Christians confess in the Apostles' Creed that they believe in "the forgiveness of sins." They believe that Jesus is their Savior because he forgives their sins. Their sins have been washed away in the waters of baptism, and they have been reconciled to God and their neighbors. In Christ they are a new creation and have a new lease on life.

A second interpretation of salvation has to do with God and the reign of God's kingdom on earth. God's kingdom has come in the person of Jesus of Nazareth, and when Jesus comes again to hand over the kingdom to the Father, there will be no more tears, suffering, and death. The principalities and powers that rule human life will be defeated, and all creation will sing doxology to the Lamb upon the throne of God. Christians who name Jesus as Savior pray in his name, "Thy kingdom come. Thy will be done, on earth as it is in heaven" (cf. Matthew 6:10).

Yet a third understanding of salvation in the Bible is not only the transformation of human beings, but also the mending of the whole of creation as well. When God's kingdom comes—finally and once for all—not only will God's peace reign among people, but also

> the wolf shall live with the lamb,
> the leopard shall lie down with the kid,
> the calf and the lion and the fatling together.
> . . . .
> The cow and the bear shall graze,
> their young shall lie down together;
> and the lion shall eat straw like the ox.
> (Isaiah 11:6–7)

And Jesus Christ shall lead them. Violence shall be no more. "They will not hurt or destroy on all my holy mountain; for the earth will be full of the knowledge of the LORD as the waters cover the sea" (11:9). Not just human beings but also the whole of creation, which "waits with eager longing" and is "groaning in labor pains," will be "set free from its bondage to decay and will obtain the freedom of the glory of the children of God" (Romans 8:19–25).

By no means are these the only interpretations of salvation and the different ways in which Jesus is Savior in the New Testament. Nor are they necessarily mutually exclusive. One might argue that what the New Testament means by salvation and the sense in which Jesus is Savior are so rich that no single image or interpretation can do justice to its mystery and depth. One attempt to capture something of both the diversity and depth of Jesus as Savior is found in John Calvin's *Institutes of the Christian Religion*. He uses the categories of prophet, priest, and king to interpret the several senses in which Jesus is the Christ, and his sixteenth-century proposal may be helpful to contemporary Christians as they seek to understand what the New Testament means by salvation.[1]

The categories of prophet, priest, and king are derived from the Old Testament. Those who held these three "offices" in ancient Israel were anointed by God, and the New Testament uses them to interpret who Jesus is. They are further evidence that Jesus Christ cannot be understood properly apart from God's covenantal history with Israel. The God who raised Jesus from the dead is the same God who led the people of Israel out of Egypt and into the promised land—the God of Abraham, Isaac, and Jacob. To know who Jesus truly is and what it means to call him the Christ is to know him as the fulfillment of Israel's covenant history with Yahweh, and the dominant figures in Israel's history are its prophets, priests, and kings. Christians confess that Jesus Christ both fulfills and redefines these three offices.

Each of these offices must be understood first in light of the Old Testament. That alone, however, is not sufficient to understand what they mean in the context of the New Testament, where they are redefined in light of the Gospels' narratives about Jesus. The three offices remind us that the full identity of Jesus as Christ and Savior can be known only by means of all three offices. Just as Jesus' identity cannot be reduced to only one part of the story that the Gospels tell (birth, ministry, death, and resurrection), so too it would be a significant mistake to understand Jesus as only prophet or as only priest or as only king. All three offices are necessary for the proper identification of him, just as all four Gospel narratives—in their entirety—are necessary in order to understand what is meant by the Christian confession that he is Christ and Savior. He is not simply one of Israel's prophets, or even the greatest of Israel's prophets. Nor is he only one of Israel's many priests, nor one of its many kings. Jesus is all three—prophet, priest, and king—and he exercises each of these offices in a unique and particular manner, redefining and giving new meaning to each.

Is Jesus a Prophet?

In chapter 2 we discussed Jesus' relation to the law of Israel and his similarities to and differences from Israel's prophets. Figures such as Samuel, Elijah, Elisha, Isaiah, Jeremiah, and Ezekiel, among others, are the bearers of God's Word to Israel. The prophets often preface their pronouncements to Israel with the words "Hear the word of the LORD of hosts" (Isaiah 39:5) or "Thus says the LORD" (Isaiah 38:1, 4). Christians believe that Jesus also speaks God's word, but not merely in the sense that his words report or repeat God's words. Jesus is not just another of Israel's prophets, not even a "first among equals." While Israel's prophets preface their pronouncements with "Thus says the LORD," Jesus of Nazareth begins his teaching by saying something that none of Israel's prophets would have dared to say. In the Sermon on the Mount in Matthew's Gospel, Jesus reminds his audience of what they are taught in God's commandments, but then he says, "But I say to you" (5:22, 28, 32, 34, 39, 44). Jesus claims an authority for himself and his words and actions that none of Israel's prophets would have claimed for themselves. And from its vantage point, after Jesus' death and resurrection, the early New Testament church makes an even more remarkable claim about him. In its Scripture and in its creeds, the church confesses that Jesus is not only a messenger and bearer of God's Word but also the very reality of God's Word in human history. As John's Gospel affirms, "And the Word became flesh and lived among us, and we have seen his glory, the glory as of a father's only son, full of grace and truth" (John 1:14). The church confesses Jesus to be not simply a man who speaks God's Word to the world, but actually the flesh-and-blood embodiment of that Word.

Jesus differs from the rest of Israel's prophets in two important respects. First, Jesus claims the authority of God for himself, and second, his acts are no less significant and no less prophetic than his words. In the first place, Jesus identifies himself with God's will or intention not only in John's Gospel, where his identification with the Word (and the identification of the Word with him) is made explicit, but in the other Gospels as well. Jesus offers himself and his ministry as a sign of God's kingdom. When John the Baptist's disciples approach Jesus and ask if he is indeed the Messiah, the long-awaited anointed one of God, Jesus does not argue his case or offer the wisdom of his teaching as a sign; rather, invoking the words of Isaiah 29:18–19, he says,

> Go and tell John what you hear and see: the blind receive their sight, the lame walk, the lepers are cleansed, the deaf hear, the dead are raised, and the poor have good news brought to them. And blessed is anyone who takes no offense at me. (Matthew 11:4–6)

Unlike the prophets, who usually direct attention away from themselves and toward Yahweh, Jesus, through his words and actions, has an authority previously unknown in the history of Israel. He does not simply pronounce God's Word to Israel; in what he says and does, he *is* God's Word.

When Calvin discusses Jesus as a prophet, he interprets him primarily as a teacher. He quotes Colossians 2:3—"in whom are hidden all the treasures of wisdom and knowledge"—and describes Jesus as teaching "perfect doctrine," which has brought an end to all prophecy, perhaps echoing Paul's words: "But as for prophecies, they will come to an end; as for tongues, they will cease; as for knowledge, it will come to an end" (1 Corinthians 13:8). Such an interpretation of the prophetic office, however, emphasizes Jesus' verbal teaching and fails to recognize the importance of the rest of his ministry. Jesus differs from the rest of Israel's prophets not only in what he says, but also in what he does. He answers

John's disciples by pointing to what he has done, and not just to what he has said. It is significant that in Luke's Gospel, Jesus begins his ministry in his hometown of Nazareth by standing in the synagogue and reading from Isaiah:

> The Spirit of the Lord is upon me,
> because he has anointed me to bring good news to the poor.
> He has sent me to proclaim release to the captives
> and recovery of sight to the blind,
> to let the oppressed go free,
> to proclaim the year of the Lord's favor.
>
> (Luke 4:18–19)

After reading, Jesus sits down and says, "Today this scripture has been fulfilled in your hearing" (4:21). It has not been fulfilled simply because Jesus has read these words from Isaiah, but because in both what he says and does, Jesus is God's Word, is God's good news, and is himself the coming of God's kingdom.

An important aspect of Jesus' teaching office is that his words are inseparable from his actions. In the narratives of the Gospels, the two are so closely related that the one cannot be adequately understood apart from the other. Jesus not only teaches about the importance of forgiving sins; he also forgives the sins of many of those who come to him, even when they do not ask him to do so. This unique feature of Jesus' prophetic office is just as important for our understanding of Jesus' church as it is for our understanding of him and the sense in which he is the Christ and the Savior. If fundamental questions about the church and its mission in the world are best answered by turning to Jesus Christ, who is Lord of the church as well as of the world, then the inseparability of word and act in Jesus' ministry has significance for our understanding of the church, the meaning of evangelism, and the church's relation to social and political institutions. The church is not an extension of the incarnation, although it is sometimes described that way in Anglican and Roman Catholic theology, but the church does seek to be faithful to the one it calls "Lord." Though neither the church nor individuals in it can ever duplicate Jesus' faithfulness to the one he calls Abba, Father, Christians are called to follow Jesus in both their personal and their social lives. That means that the church must strive to make its teaching and proclamation consistent with what it says and does. And vice versa. It is not acceptable for the church to restrict its ministry to proclamation. In the New Testament, proclamation is not merely the act of preaching; it is also acts of witness and ministry. A church that is faithful to Jesus Christ cannot simply preach good news to the poor and release to the captives. It must also be involved in the liberation of the poor and oppressed from their bondage. The church is committed to ministries of compassion not because it identifies the gospel with a particular political party, movement, or ideology, but because the Lord it follows calls his disciples to serve him in behalf of "the least of these" (Matthew 25:45).

In the words of John's Gospel, Jesus is "the way, and the truth, and the life" (14:6), not because of the unusual wisdom of his teaching, nor because of the truthfulness of his acts, but because what he says perfectly coheres with what he does, and both what he says and does are faithful and obedient to the one he calls Abba and to God's kingdom. In the narratives of the Gospels, Jesus redefines the office of prophet, and in so doing he illumines the meaning of faith. In his person and in what he does, Jesus reveals faith to be both unreserved trust and perfect obedience. As the faithful prophet, Jesus trusts completely in God's grace and faithfulness, exhibits perfect obedience in proclaiming and enacting God's kingdom, and offers a sign of that kingdom—a sign discernible to the eyes of faith—in his person and actions.

The stories of Jesus' temptation by the devil in Matthew 4:1–11 and Luke 4:1–13 are descriptions of Jesus' wholehearted trust in God and obedience to God. The tempter offers Jesus a number of ways to be unfaithful to the one he calls Abba. After forty days and nights of fasting, Jesus, like Israel in the wilderness (Exodus 16), is famished. He suffers the most basic human need: daily bread. And so Satan tempts him to satisfy this elemental need. If he truly is the Son of God, then surely he can turn stones into bread (Matthew 4:3–4). In response, Jesus quotes Scripture from Deuteronomy 8:3: "One does not live by bread alone, but by every word that comes from the mouth of God." The most elemental human need is not bread, but God.

And so the devil tries a second time, only this time he adds the Bible to his argument (Matthew 4:5–7). He takes Jesus to "the pinnacle of the temple" in Jerusalem. If he is truly the Son of God, he should throw himself to the ground, for Scripture says God will command his angels to protect him (Psalm 91:11–12). Jesus responds by quoting Deuteronomy 6:16: "Do not put the Lord your God to the test." This is not the last time Jesus will face this temptation. As he is dying on Golgotha's cross, the chief priests, scribes, elders, and the bandits crucified beside him taunt him: "He trusts in God; let God deliver him now, if he wants to; for he said, 'I am God's Son'" (Matthew 27:43). To test God, however, is not to trust God. And Jesus will trust God in all things—even in his dying.

Finally, the devil takes Jesus to "a very high mountain" (Matthew is fond of mountains) and offers him the power and the splendor of the kingdoms of this world if only he will "fall down and worship" him (4:8–10). The tempter does not ask Jesus to deny or renounce God, only to expand the number of those he worships. Jesus, however, is interested in a different kingdom than what Satan offers. Once again, he who is the Word quotes words from Deuteronomy 6:13: "Worship the Lord your God, and serve only him." Not only does Jesus quote these words to Satan; he also embodies and enacts them.

The Gospel narratives identify Jesus as the faithful prophet who not only reveals the true meaning of faith but also calls his disciples and his church to be faithful, to trust and obey only God. In the Gospels, Jesus' journey begins in the wilderness of his temptations, at the beginning of his ministry, and concludes in the bleak wilderness of Golgotha. From the beginning to the end of this journey, Jesus, in the words of the Epistle to the Hebrews, is "the pioneer and perfecter of our faith, who for the sake of the joy that was set before him endured the cross, disregarding its shame, and has taken his seat at the right hand of the throne of God" (12:2). As the faithful prophet, Jesus calls his church to pay attention to both what he says and does, for in their relation to one another, they constitute the one Word of God. Jesus' prophetic office is indispensable for who he is, the sense in which he is "Savior" of the world, and what his church is called to be and do. He exercises his prophetic office in his teaching and ministry. This is not just any teaching and not just any form of ministry. Jesus presents God's kingdom to those in society who are without hope, and what he says and does is finally vindicated by God in Jesus' resurrection. In the words of A Brief Statement of Faith,

> God raised this Jesus from the dead,
> vindicating his sinless life,
> breaking the power of sin and evil,
> delivering us from death to life eternal.[2]

As the prophet of God's kingdom, Jesus is the faithful one. But what does this faithful prophet have to do with us? Scripture does not separate faith in Jesus Christ from the response of faithful discipleship on the part of those who hear his words, witness what he does, and choose to follow him. To confess that "Jesus is Lord" is at the same time to follow Jesus, and to follow Jesus, in his words, is to take up a cross: "If any want to become my followers, let them deny themselves and take up their cross and follow me" (Mark 8:34). A church in which there is much profession of faith but little evidence of discipleship is not a church that takes Jesus Christ or the gospel seriously. As T. S. Eliot reminds us in his Choruses from "The Rock":

> Our age is an age of moderate virtue
> And of moderate vice
> When men will not lay down the Cross
> Because they will never assume it
> Yet nothing is impossible, nothing,
> To men of faith and conviction.[3]

The Jesus of the New Testament is anything but a man of moderation. Jesus' invitation to take up and cross and follow him is neither "practical" nor reasonable nor an act of moderation: "You will be dragged before governors and kings because of me" (Matthew 10:18). Any church whose members understand themselves to be disciples of and witnesses to Jesus the Prophet cannot evade the difficult question of discipleship—not only what it meant in the middle of the first century, but also what it means at the beginning of the twenty-first century and what crosses Jesus' followers are being asked to shoulder today.

How Does Jesus Save?

The New Testament often refers to Jesus as a priest. He is a priest in the tradition of ancient Israel's priests, but Jesus also differs from them in some important ways. One New Testament text that emphasizes Jesus' priestly office is the Letter to the Hebrews, which describes Jesus as "a high priest, holy, blameless, undefiled, separated from sinners, and exalted above the heavens" (7:26).

Like priests in the Old Testament, Jesus mediates between God and sinful people. The term "mediator" has often been used in Christian theology to describe what it means to say that Jesus is Savior. What is a mediator? In a labor dispute or legal arbitration, a good mediator enables two parties in a conflict to better understand one another and to reconcile their differences. In Christian faith, Jesus is the incomparable mediator. He is the reality and the presence of God's love and grace in the world; in the language of the Letter to the Ephesians, Jesus "has broken down the dividing wall, that is, the hostility between us" (2:14). Jesus overcomes the broken relationship between God and sinful humanity and the divisions that separate human beings from one another. He is able to do that because Christian faith confesses him to be fully and truly human. In the words of the Epistle to the Hebrews, "one who in every respect has been tested as we are, yet without sin" (4:15). If he were not one of us, Jesus would not be the embodiment and the enactment of God's forgiveness in human life and history. God's grace would then be an interesting idea, but not a reality in human history. Christian faith might be a philosophy but not a material, tangible reality. On the other hand, if he were not "without sin," Jesus could not do for a sinful world what it cannot do for itself. As mediator, he who was without sin "assumes" or "takes" human sin on himself and mediates God's grace and forgiveness to sinners.

In human experience a mediator is often understood to be a disinterested third party, who identifies with neither of the parties in the dispute. It is this third-party status that enables the mediator to be impartial and neutral. Jesus Christ is not that kind of mediator. He is a mediator like no other in that he identifies fully with both the holy, righteous one he calls "Father" and with sinful humanity. He represents the one to the other because he is at one and the same time both. In the classical language of the church, which we will examine in the following chapter, Jesus of Nazareth as the Christ is one person who is both truly and fully human: truly human in that he is undistorted by sin, and truly and fully the embodiment of God's glory, grace, and truth (John 1:14).

In the Old Testament, because of human sin a priest presents humanity's sacrifices and pleas for forgiveness to God, who is holy, righteous, and just. But God is also merciful and extends forgiveness to a repentant people. Jesus performs his high-priestly office in much the same way as did Israel's high priests: "Every high priest chosen from among mortals is put in charge of things pertaining to God on their behalf, to offer gifts and sacrifices for sins" (Hebrews 5:1). On behalf of his people, the priest offers gifts and sacrifices to atone for human sin. Jesus does the same. He is, says Hebrews, "a high priest forever according to the order of Melchizedek" (6:20; see also 5:5–6; 7:1–28). Like Melchizedek, who according to Psalm 110:4 is "a priest forever," so too Jesus' priesthood is eternal.

But Jesus also differs from the priests of the Old Testament in several important ways. First, although Jesus sympathizes with humanity's sinfulness, he is himself without sin. Like Israel's priests, Jesus represents sinful humanity before God, yet he differs from them in that he is faithful to God and "unblemished" by sin. Second, Jesus is not a priest by birth. He exercises his office as priest not by inheritance but because he has been anointed by God to be the mediator between God and the world. Third, like Israel's priests, Jesus offers sacrifices to God for human sins, but his sacrifice is not the blood of animals or the gifts of the people: it is the sacrifice of himself crucified. He offers the blood of the cross and the gift of himself. Finally, according to the Epistle to the Hebrews, Jesus continually intercedes for humanity before God, but the sacrifice of the cross was sufficient once and for all and need never be repeated: "Unlike the other high priests, he has no need to offer sacrifices day after day, first for his own sins, and then for those of the people; he did this once for all when he offered himself" (7:27).

Like Israel's priests, Jesus' activity can be summarized by a single word: atonement. Literally, it means at-one-ment, and it is a familiar word to many Jews and Christians, so familiar it is sometimes taken for granted. Yet let us recognize what the word presupposes. It assumes something that not all people may agree with—that human beings are not "at one" with one another and, even more important, not "at one" with God. The human condition is marked by alienation and estrangement between people and between humanity and God. What humanity most desperately needs, therefore, is to overcome this estrangement, to rediscover peace with God and therein peace among themselves. For Christian faith, Jesus Christ is the high priest who accomplishes this mediation, who reconciles sinners to God and to one another. His atonement makes them "one." He represents sinful humanity before God and extends to them the grace, mercy, and forgiveness of God. And because he represents all humanity, sinners are reconciled not only to God but also to one another.

Christian faith has sometimes been described in terms of two basic realities: the reality of human sin on the one hand, and God's grace and forgiveness in Jesus Christ on the other. Atonement is an important term in Christian faith because it describes how God's grace in Christ overcomes the despair of human sin. As we have seen, one of the most vivid statements of this despair is the cry of the apostle Paul: "Wretched man that I am! Who will rescue me from this body of death?" (Romans 7:24). And in the following verse, Paul proclaims the good news: "Thanks be to God through Jesus Christ our Lord!" What has happened? How does Paul account for this miraculous transition from despair to new life? He does so by pointing to Jesus' cross. He tells the Christians in Corinth, "For I decided to know nothing among you except Jesus Christ, and him crucified" (1 Corinthians 2:2).

In order to explain how Paul gets from verse 24 to verse 25 in Romans 7, from despair to forgiveness, the New Testament employs a diverse array of images to interpret Jesus' death—ransom, debt repaid, sacrifice, victory over evil, and many others. Over the centuries, theologians have taken the events of Jesus' life and death, especially his death by crucifixion, and have interpreted them by means of this array of images and metaphors. Jesus' atoning death has sometimes been interpreted as a cosmic battle fought between God and the devil, in which the devil is tricked by the frail humanity of Jesus. The devil consumes Jesus on the cross but is then defeated by Jesus in his resurrection. Sometimes described as the *Christus Victor* theory, this interpretation emphasizes the sense in which the cross is a triumph over not only sin, but even over evil itself.

A second set of interpretations, sometimes described as satisfaction or substitution theories and often attributed to the eleventh-century theologian Anselm, employs images that describe the cross as a ransom for sin or the repayment of an impossible debt. Examples are Jesus' saying in Mark 10:45 that the Son of man "came not to be served but to serve, and to give his life a ransom for many"; and Paul's words to the Christians in Corinth that they do not belong to themselves because they have been "bought with a price" (1 Corinthians 6:20). Because of its sinfulness, humanity owes a just and righteous God a debt or restitution that it can never provide. Out of sheer love, God then does for a sinful world what it cannot do for itself: "For God so loved the world that he gave his only Son, so that everyone who believes in him may not perish but may have eternal life" (John 3:16). Jesus Christ takes the place of sinful humanity, bears the violence of the cross, and in so doing removes the sin that separates sinners from God and one another. In both of these interpretations, humanity finds itself in an impossible situation because of its sin: as unrighteous people in bondage to evil, and deserving nothing but judgment and punishment from a righteous God.

Yet a third interpretation, often associated with Abelard, another eleventh-century theologian, locates the problem not in human bondage to evil or in human unrighteousness, but in the human heart and imagination. The consequences of sin are such that human beings no longer love God or neighbor. But the power of the cross, as the ultimate demonstration of God's love, is its power to transform human hearts and minds. Sometimes described as "the moral influence theory," this interpretation focuses less on cosmic evil or the satisfaction of God's righteousness and the repayment of a massive debt and more on the power of God's love to change hearts and minds.

There are some common themes in these different interpretations of atonement, but also some important differences. Each of them understands humanity's estrangement from God and neighbor to be a condition that human beings are unable to remedy and to which God's response is Jesus' death and resurrection. Where they differ is in their interpretations of how human sin is overcome by the cross and how it transforms sinners' relationships to God and to one another. These three interpretations—cosmic conflict, satisfaction/substitution, and moral influence—are not the only ways Christians have understood how Jesus' cross is salvific. Each of them reflects the cultural contexts and worldviews in which they first emerged. There is both something that is right about their respective interpretations of Jesus as Savior and also something that seems inadequate about each of them. In the *Christus Victor* and satisfaction theories, for example, human beings seem at best to be spectators and uninvolved in the drama of salvation. The moral influence theory, on the other hand, seems to make human beings the primary agent in salvation and minimizes human captivity to the power of sin.

As is often the case when Scripture uses multiple images to describe something—be it God, Jesus Christ, sin, or the church—the reason for this diversity is that the holy mystery to which the Bible witnesses is such that no single image and no single interpretation can ever be wholly adequate. The meaning of the cross, after all, is what Paul describes in Romans 5:15–17 as "the free gift" of God's grace in Jesus Christ. The very nature of that "free gift" is surely beyond the reach of every human attempt to account for it or explain it. It should not be surprising that if Paul describes Jesus' cross as "foolishness," all attempts to capture the sense in which that cross is "unto salvation" will also finally seem inadequate.

Do we have to believe in a particular theory of the atonement in order to be a Christian? Is there such a thing as *the* Christian doctrine of the atonement? The multiplicity of images used in the New Testament to describe the atonement suggests that just as no single image is entirely adequate, so too no single theory or doctrine will suffice. Each makes a contribution to our understanding of how Jesus' life and death are, in the words of the Nicene Creed, "for our salvation." C. S. Lewis observed that before he became a Christian he "was under the impression that the first thing Christians had to believe was one particular theory as to what the point of this [Christ's] dying was." After he became a Christian he learned this impression was not true:

> What I came to see later on was that neither this theory nor any other is Christianity. The central Christian belief is that Christ's death has somehow put us right with God and given us a fresh start. Theories as to how it did this are another matter.[4]

That is not to say that theories and doctrine are unimportant. Theology is always faith in search of understanding; for the sake of the gospel, it is important we understand as fully as possible that which faith confesses. At the same time we must not confuse the centrality of Christ's death for Christian faith and the reality of God's grace and forgiveness with the tentativeness and partial truthfulness of human theories and doctrines.

What do Christians mean by their claim that Jesus' work as priest is that of at-one-ment, of reconciling sinners to God? In order to understand how Jesus redefines the Old Testament office of priest, we must look carefully at the Gospel narratives' description of him. Jesus' death cannot be properly understood apart from his ministry: the kingdom of God that he proclaims, teaches, enacts, and embodies. Nor can the cross be properly understood in Christian faith apart from the resurrection. The crucified Jesus is the one whom God raises from the dead. Jesus' priesthood is not intelligible apart from his identity as both prophet and king. And yet, as is evident in the Epistle to the Hebrews, it is Jesus' death on the cross that is the basis for Christian interpretations of atonement and reconciliation.

Just as it is a mistake to separate the meaning of Jesus' death from his prophetic ministry, so too his death has no significance apart from the Easter claim that God raised him from the dead. Unfortunate things happen to Christian faith if it forgets that the good news of Easter is about the horror of the cross. Christian faith cannot emphasize the glory and joy of Easter and neglect the darkness and despair of Good Friday. If it does so, it takes human sin less seriously than the Gospels do, misrepresents the reality of evil, and minimizes the costly love of the cross. On the other hand, faith cannot concentrate only on Good Friday and ignore Easter. To do so would be to make the cross a martyr's heroic but yet tragic and ultimately meaningless death. In Christian faith, the resurrection is always the resurrection of the crucified One, and the crucifixion is always the vicious execution of the one whom God raises from the dead and reveals to be God's chosen and anointed Christ.

The cross always points to the resurrection, and the resurrection presupposes the horrible reality of the cross, but it is the cross that defines Jesus' activity as priest and serves as the basis for the atonement. An interpretation of Christian faith that ignores Jesus' teaching and ministry as his prophetic office, or that ignores the resurrection as his royal office—that interpretation is impoverished. Nonetheless, all sound Christian theology begins and ends at the foot of the cross. It is the single event in the Gospels that unveils the full depth and horror of human sin and the radical nature of God's grace and love. Human sin manifests itself in many different ways, but its most devastating form is a self-centered life cut off from the world and other people. This virulent form of pride and selfishness feeds on fear, loves the darkness of isolation, and fears the bright light of truth. Pride and fear go hand in hand, and the one reality they cannot tolerate is their opposite—a love, derived from being loved by God, that seeks other people's fulfillment and happiness. Jesus may have been executed because the leaders of the temple feared that he threatened public order, and the Romans may have crucified him because they feared that he posed a threat to their rule. But the real opposition Jesus encountered and that led to the cross was pride rooted in power and fueled by fear.

In the Gospels' narratives, what is striking about Jesus is his remarkable freedom, not only in relation to long-established traditions and institutions, but also in his relations to other people. Freely and unreservedly he enters into relations with all kinds of people, some of whom were considered unacceptable by many in society. Jesus seeks the company of lepers, the mentally deranged, those possessed by demons, prostitutes, tax collectors, Roman soldiers and administrators, the poor and the rich. He approaches them with acceptance and affirmation, not with reproach. He heals, casts out demons, forgives, and restores. He restores sinners to community. There appear to be no limits to Jesus' love. In Luke's Gospel, Jesus not only tells a story about a shepherd who will travel as far as necessary to find a lost sheep (Luke 15:3–7); Jesus also travels the long road from Galilee to Jerusalem (9:51–19:28) in order to save the lost sheep of Israel. It is this life-giving love that evokes fear and hatred from those who cling to an established order and the power it provides them. Historically, Jesus was executed by an occupying Roman government; in reality, he was killed by a sinful world that hates what it fears, clings to established order, and cannot tolerate a love that exposes its pride and power to be contrary to what God intends for the world.

Jesus is the high priest of Christian faith because his cross is the ultimate act of human love in the face of the world's selfishness, fear, and hatred. However, it is not just the bare historical fact of his death that makes Jesus the mediator and his cross the means of atonement and reconciliation between a righteous and loving God and a sinful world. Thousands were crucified by the Romans in the first century. Jesus was by no means the only person who endured the pain and suffering of crucifixion. Many people in human history—Socrates, Abraham Lincoln, Martin Luther King Jr., to name only a few—lived exemplary lives, lives that seem to represent the noblest aspects of what it means to be human, but few, if any, Christians would say, "Socrates (or Lincoln or King) died for my sins, and is my savior." Christians confess that Jesus of Nazareth is the one high priest who alone has atoned for human sin and reconciled the world to God. They make that confession because in both his ministry and his death, Jesus is what no other human being has been and can be: the one who loves God fully and freely and reflects that love in his relationships to other people and the world. In the Jesus of the Gospels, there is no self-centeredness, no incoherence between what he says and does, which is what the Letter to the Hebrews means by its claim that he is like us in every respect, yet without sinning (2:17; 4:15).

Jesus' cross overcomes what the Letter to the Ephesians describes as "the dividing wall" of hostility between sinful people (2:14). He repairs or "heals" the breach that separates sinners from God and human beings from one another. That estrangement is created by selfish human beings, who are unable to live fully and completely before God and with one another. Jesus is not just a moral or even religious *example* of unselfish, self-giving love—what the New Testament describes as *agapē*. In what he says and does—in his person—and above all in his cross, he *is* the reality of *agapē*: its embodiment and enactment. He is not an example, one instance among many, of some general notion of love. God's love is the particular life that Jesus lives. The astounding claim made by the New Testament is that the death of this first-century Jew in a remote, backwater portion of the Roman Empire has forever altered the world and the relation of human beings to God and to their neighbors.

As the high priest of Christian faith, Jesus Christ discloses the meaning of atonement by making that peculiar form of love that

Christians refer to as *agapē* a reality in both his life and his death. Christians are not called by Jesus to carry his cross or to endure his death. They are called to allow the power of the cross to manifest itself in their personal and communal existence. The good news that Christians proclaim is not just that God has overcome sin by means of Jesus' cross, but that his cross has reconciled and will reconcile "all things" by unleashing the power of *agapē* in the world.

Why Do Christians Call Jesus "Lord"?

Jesus is not only prophet and priest: he is also king. As with his offices of prophet and priest, so too his royal office is continuous with Israel's kings; yet in the context of the Gospels' narratives, he also redefines the meaning of that office. Like Israel's kings, Jesus also is anointed by God. Being anointed as king was a sign of having been chosen by God. Although Israel did not understand its kings to be deity, it did hold them in high esteem. When given the chance to kill Saul, David refused to do so, saying, "Do not destroy him; for who can raise his hand against the LORD's anointed, and be guiltless?" (1 Samuel 26:9). The king bears God's blessing and consequently must be treated with dignity and respect. In the New Testament, Jesus was also anointed, like Saul and David. The Gospels report that at his baptism by John the Baptist, a dove descended on Jesus and a voice from heaven declared, "This is my Son, the Beloved, with whom I am well pleased" (Matthew 3:17). However, although he is anointed by God, like the rest of Israel's kings, Jesus also differs from them in the way in which he rules and in the nature of his kingdom. Jesus is not just an instrument of God's righteousness and rule; as God's anointed one, he is the presence and promise of God's kingdom in human history.

It is not Jesus' baptism that established him as king: the dramatic event that Christians call "resurrection" is the basis for the foundational Christian confession that "Jesus is Lord." What Christians mean when they make that claim can only be understood by examining the Gospels' narratives in their entirety, especially from the perspective of the church's Easter faith and experience.

If Jesus' story had concluded with the Gospels' accounts of his crucifixion, then he might be a tragic figure of mythic proportions, but he would not be the one whom Christians call "Lord." He would be, like Socrates, only yet another good person who came to a bad end. And if the final event in the Jesus story were Golgotha and the tomb of Joseph of Arimathea, it would be difficult to understand what enabled his disciples to overcome their fear and despair, reassemble, and begin a ministry that would take them to what at that time were the ends of the earth and would lead many of them to suffering, persecution, and execution. The strange experience that Christians refer to as "Easter" is the foundation of their claim that "Jesus is Lord," God's anointed one, the Christ, and that the forgiveness of sin and the power of sacrificial love are now realities in the world.

Precisely what Christians mean by "resurrection," or for that matter what the Bible means by the term, is not always clear or at least not as clear as some might wish. Once again, we have a case where the meaning of an event is more important to Scripture than the precision of its details. In its simplest form the problem is that no one witnessed the resurrection. In the New Testament, two sets of stories are the basis for the claim that God raised Jesus from the dead. One set of stories, such as we find summarized in almost creedal form in 1 Corinthians 15:3–7, describes a series of appearances of Jesus—who has been crucified, dead, and buried—to his disciples, followers, and friends. The reality of these appearances of the dead Jesus, now miraculously alive, was so overwhelming that it led those who witnessed them to conclude that God had raised Jesus from the dead, and in so doing God had triumphed over the forces of sin, death, and evil. In order to interpret these experiences of a crucified but now living Jesus, Jesus' followers uttered the word "resurrection." It was not a word they made up. Almost all of Jesus' early disciples and followers were Jewish, and "resurrection" is a term deeply rooted in the Old Testament and in the faith of Israel. From its beginning, Israel experienced God's bringing life out of death. Israel was in bondage as slave labor in Egypt, but God miraculously brought life out of death by freeing Israel from the Egyptians. So too Israel wandered in the wilderness until God miraculously brought them into a land flowing with milk and honey. And the apocalyptic literature of Daniel includes texts that promise a time when "your people shall be delivered, everyone who is found written in the book." When that happens, "many of those who sleep in the dust of the earth shall awake, some to everlasting life, and some to shame and everlasting contempt" (12:1–2). Texts such as these enabled Jesus' followers to interpret the experience of his presence, following his death, by means of resurrection. The only problem is that Jewish apocalyptic knows nothing of the resurrection of a single person, but only a resurrection of all those who sleep in the dust of the earth. The startling surprise for Jesus' disciples was that only one person, Jesus, was raised. Christians, like Paul, concluded that Jesus' resurrection was the "first fruits" of what was yet to come: "the resurrection of [all] the dead" (1 Corinthians 15:12–23). On the basis of these appearance stories, many people in early Christian communities eagerly looked forward to that day in which God would disclose to the world that Jesus is the Christ and that his kingdom has come in power and glory.

In addition to the appearance stories, a second set of stories describes the experience of some of the women who visit his tomb on the third day after his burial. The accounts vary as to which women go; what they discover is that Jesus is not in the tomb. In Mark's Gospel they find a young man dressed in a white robe, sitting in the tomb. He tells them that Jesus is risen, and the women respond, not by joyfully singing the "Hallelujah Chorus," but by fleeing from the tomb "for terror and amazement had seized them; and they said nothing to anyone, for they were afraid" (16:8).

To what, then, does the term "resurrection" refer? Does it refer only to the appearances of Jesus to his followers and disciples? The apostle Paul, who in 1 Corinthians 15 gives us the first written interpretation of the resurrection, apparently knows nothing of a story about an empty tomb (see 15:3–7). Or does the term "resurrection" refer to the claim by Jesus' followers that his tomb was empty? And if the latter, what became of Jesus' body? How was it "raised," and where was it raised to? The Bible does not tell us what happened inside Jesus' tomb. What it does say is that Jesus' disciples had various experiences following his death that led them to a threefold confession: that God raised Jesus from the dead; that in so doing God revealed him to be the Christ, the anointed one, who establishes God's kingdom of justice and righteousness; and that this Jesus will one day destroy evil and reign over a new heaven and a new earth.

In the Bible the early church was unwilling—or more likely, unable—to say precisely what happened at the resurrection. It could only report the experiences that led it to confess that God raised Jesus from the dead. What mattered to those early Christians was not how such an event was possible. It was possible because God did it. What mattered was the significance of that event for Jesus' identity. In raising Jesus from the dead, God vindicated Jesus' proclamation of the nearness of the kingdom and God's faithfulness. God not only vindicated him but also revealed him to be Lord and Christ, the very reality of the kingdom itself.

His resurrection establishes Jesus as Lord. That does not mean that Jesus only becomes Lord on Easter morning. In the words of A Declaration of Faith,

> Jesus is Lord!
> He has been Lord from the beginning.
> He will be Lord at the end.
> Even now he is Lord.[5]

It is in the light of Easter that Jesus' followers know for the first time who he truly is. But because of who he is, they know that from the beginning he has been Christ, Savior, Lord. As the Word made flesh, to use the language of the Gospel of John (1:1, 14 RSV), he was in the beginning. Or as the hymn in the first chapter of Colossians puts it, "He is the image of the invisible God, the firstborn of all creation; for in him all things in heaven and on earth were created; . . . all things have been created through him and for him" (1:15–16). It is Easter and the conviction that God raised Jesus from the dead that enabled the early church to confess that Jesus is Lord.

Jesus exercises his lordship, his royal office, in a unique way. The kingship that he proclaims and enacts differs from that of all the other kings whom the world has known. "Jesus is Lord" means that he reigns over "all things," to use the language of Colossians (1:15–20). All things are subject to him, including every principality and power. But Jesus does not reign by sheer unlimited power. The power of God, Paul tells the Corinthians, is not the power of Caesar, but the weakness of the cross, the weakness of suffering love. Jesus "reigns" by the power of sacrificial and self-giving love, which triumphs over all things because of his resurrection. In the imagery of John's vision in Revelation (5:12), innumerable living creatures surrounding God's throne sing,

> Worthy is the lamb that was slaughtered
> to receive power and wealth and wisdom and might
> and honor and glory and blessing!

Jesus reigns and exercises power in a fundamentally different way than all of Rome's Caesars and all other worldly powers. He reigns not by brute strength but by means of a love that never lets go and that persists even in the darkness of death and nothingness. Just as the cross must not be interpreted apart from the resurrection, so too the resurrection must always be understood in relation to the cross. The Jesus whom God raised from the dead is the Crucified One, and in his royal office as Lord of all things, he does not cease to be the Crucified One as he reigns in his kingdom.

Jesus' identity as the Christ has been established once and for all time by the resurrection, and God's kingdom is a reality in him. That is not, however, the end of the story that the Bible tells about Jesus. According to Luke, after blessing his disciples at Bethany, the resurrected Christ was then "carried up into heaven" (Luke 24:50–53; Acts 1:1–11), and the Apostles' Creed affirms that he who was crucified, dead, buried, and descended into hell was also raised from the dead on the third day and then ascended into heaven, where he sits "on the right hand of God the Father Almighty; from thence he shall come to judge the quick [that is, living] and the dead." The Bible insists that the kingdom that has drawn near in Jesus, the apocalyptic prophet and high priest, is also yet to be. Although Jesus has been vindicated, God's kingdom has become a reality in him, and the power of evil and death have been broken, the world still awaits the final realization of the kingdom, when in the language of the hymn in the second chapter of Philippians, every knee will bend "in heaven and on earth and under the earth" and every tongue confess "that Jesus Christ is Lord, to the glory of God the Father" (2:10–11). Jesus' identity is no longer in doubt, but his story is unfinished. According to Luke's account in Acts, it continues in the life and missionary work of his disciples. Jesus reigns, but he is also yet to reign, and his narrative is unfinished until "all things" are brought to God through him (1 Corinthians 15:28).

It is as the crucified king that Jesus gives Christian hope its distinctive shape and meaning. In Jesus' office as prophet, Christians discern what faith is, what it means to truly trust in God. In his office as priest, Christians see something of the wonder and depth of God's suffering love. Thus also, in Jesus' royal office, his identity as Lord of lords and King of kings, Christians know the meaning of Christian hope. This hope is neither wishful thinking nor the spirit of optimism nor speculation about the future. Because God has vindicated Jesus by raising him from the dead, Christians look to the future not in quiet desperation or grim determination, but in confident anticipation that the future, although unknown, belongs to the God whose faithfulness has been made clear in Jesus' resurrection. Christians do not know what the future holds, but they do know that the future belongs to God and that God has and will fulfill God's promises in Jesus Christ, who was Lord in the beginning, will be Lord at the end, and "even now is Lord." They can face an unknown future because they know that God is faithful and that Jesus is Lord. And because Jesus reigns, Christians need not fear what is yet to be. Christian hope does not mean that Christians know what awaits them or the world in the future. Christian hope is neither a denial of the reality of death nor an affirmation of the immortality of the soul. In the words of the apostle Paul, what Christian hope does affirm is the hope found in one's baptism: "If we live, we live to the Lord, and if we die, we die to the Lord; so then, whether we live or whether we die, we are the Lord's" (Romans 14:8).

For Christians, the confession that Jesus is Lord has never been only a religious claim. Some Christians have occasionally tried to separate its theological meaning from its political significance, but they have been able to do that only by distorting its biblical meaning. The conviction that Jesus is Lord over all things has enabled Christians through the ages to deny the competing claims of "lordship" from all other pretenders—not only Caesars, tyrants, and other repressive governments, but even the church, and death itself. The Scots Confession was written by Christians in the sixteenth century in response to the claims of "lordship" made by the Roman Catholic Church and the thrones of France and England. Its first sentence declares, "We confess and acknowledge one God alone, to whom alone we cleave, whom alone we must serve, whom only we must worship, and in whom alone we put our trust."[6] Nearly four centuries later, Christians in Germany faced the rising tide of the Nazi government and in the Theological Declaration of Barmen declared, "Jesus Christ, as he is attested for us in Holy Scripture, is the one Word of God which we have to hear and which we have to trust and obey in life and in death."[7] The confession "Jesus is Lord" means that he and he alone is the one whom Christians trust, love, and in whom they have hope.

The offices of prophet, priest, and king illumine the person and work—the identity—of Jesus of Nazareth and the meaning of life lived in him, but they do so only when they are used to interpret the stories in the Bible that give Jesus his full and true identity. He is the faithful prophet who proclaims and enacts in his person and ministry the coming of God's kingdom.

Chapter Four

What Did the Early Christians Believe about Jesus?

In chapter 2 we recognized that Jesus' true identity is a central concern, perhaps *the* concern, of the New Testament. The question that Jesus asks Peter in Mark 8:29, "But who do you say that I am?" is addressed to every reader of Mark's Gospel. It is a question asked of every Christian and every church. Christians through the ages have responded to that question just as Peter did—by confessing that Jesus is the Messiah, the Christ. But they have interpreted the title of *Christos*, or Messiah, in many ways. What are we to make of these differences? Dietrich Bonhoeffer rephrased the question posed in Mark 8 as "Who is Jesus Christ for us today?" Why did he add the words "for us today"? Is not Jesus Christ "the same yesterday and today and forever" (Hebrews 13:8)?

As Christians found themselves in new and different cultural contexts, facing difficult problems unknown to those who preceded them, they discovered that it was not enough simply to repeat Scripture. Like their predecessors they turned to the Bible for guidance, but they also found that they had to reinterpret the witness of Scripture in response to new contexts and challenges. Repeatedly churches developed new forms of language, new theological paradigms, and new creeds and confessions in order to answer the question concerning Jesus' identity. It has not been a fascination with novelty that has prompted churches to develop new ways of saying who Jesus is, but an evangelical commitment to the proclamation of the gospel in a language that the rest of society can understand and that directly addresses the new issues and challenges before the church. Indeed, the history of Christian theology can be understood as showing the various ways individuals and churches across the centuries have answered the question concerning Jesus' identity.

Why Do Christians Write Creeds about Jesus?

In the first five centuries of the Christian era, there were numerous disagreements about the identity of Jesus of Nazareth. To many people today those historical arguments sound distant, tedious, and unnecessary. It is not always clear why these subtle theological debates mattered, why they were relevant to the life of the church then, or why they are relevant to Christians today. Furthermore, many of those involved in these debates were passionate about their convictions and in the name of Jesus Christ did cruel things to other Christians. In the fourth century, Athanasius was banished five times from Alexandria. A thousand years later, in 1553, John Calvin was involved in the execution by burning of Michael Servetus because of his attack on the doctrine of the Trinity. Many people have difficulty understanding how Christians could have done such terrible things to one another in the name of Jesus Christ. Although we cannot excuse what they did, the intensity of their convictions about the identity and significance of Jesus may stand in striking contrast to the indifference with which some Christians today discuss similar questions.

Some of the most important debates in the development of the early church's understanding of Jesus as the Christ (what is sometimes referred to as "classical Christology") took place in the fourth and fifth centuries. Why were these debates about Jesus so important to the early church, and why do they continue to matter today? Here are three reasons. First, most of those involved in these early controversies recognized that the central issue was the very heart of the gospel. The reason why Christians expended such enormous amounts of time, intellectual energy, and passion in these debates about Jesus was that they believed the stakes were very high—nothing less than their conviction that Jesus was God's anointed one and the agent of salvation. No matter how obscure and irrelevant these ancient debates may sound to Christians today, in almost every case what fueled the fire (figuratively) was a genuine concern on all sides that Christian faith in Jesus Christ not be misrepresented and that salvation not be misinterpreted. What was at stake (literally and figuratively) was not just what Christians believed but also how they thought they were suppose to live as people who were a "new creation" in Jesus Christ.

Second, these were not simply intellectual debates between theologians, but also issues related to the church's role in its larger society. And these larger political and social contexts played an important role in determining the outcome of these debates. Theological controversies about the sense in which Jesus is and is not the Christ, the chosen one of God, and his relation to the Father, or first person of the Trinity—these were significant not only for theologians but also for the church's life in its larger culture. And the same is true today. Although contemporary Christians live in cultures vastly different from those of the fourth and fifth centuries, they too are influenced by the political issues that surround them: what they confess about the identity and significance of Jesus as the Christ should have implications for their social and political decisions as well.

Finally, what may strike the contemporary reader as major weaknesses in the early church's creeds—for example, obscure and archaic language such as "same substance" and "two natures"—may actually be their greatest strength. There is no such thing as a timeless creed, one that is written for all times, places, and situations. The church's creeds, like its Scriptures, were written at specific times in particular places, in response to questions about the meaning of Christian faith and discipleship. In order to answer those questions responsibly and faithfully, the church found it necessary to confess its faith in language that would be intelligible to its surrounding society and culture. In the fourth and fifth centuries, the dominant cultures around the Mediterranean were Greek and Roman, and not surprisingly, the church formulated its confession about Jesus as the Christ in Latin and Greek and in the categories of those cultures. Although terms such as "substance" and "nature" may sound to us like a strange way to describe a person's identity, they were not strange to the Latin- and Greek-speaking cultures of the fourth and fifth centuries. This was familiar language to them. One way to understand "modern" Christology (Christology as it has developed in the nineteenth and later centuries) is as the search by Christians for new language and an alternative paradigm to that of the early church. Just as Christians in the fourth and fifth centuries had to find appropriate language to speak about Christ in their context, so too churches today must find language that is clear and intelligible to them. That cannot be done simply by repeating the Bible or what Christians said in the fourth and fifth centuries, although there are still valuable lessons that can be learned from them. If Christians today wish to avoid the mistakes and blind alleys of the early church, they would be wise to listen to those ancient creeds and confessions and learn from them.

In the church's first five centuries, there were many discussions of Jesus' relation to the one he called "Abba" or "Father" and the sense in which Jesus is and is not the Christ. Although we cannot discuss all of them, it is important that we review the major issues and figures in these debates.[1]

As we have seen in the previous chapter, interpretations of Jesus as the Christ are vitally important for Christian faith because Christians believe that he reveals the meaning and reality of salvation. Most debates about Jesus are debates about what Christians mean when they call him "Savior." In even the most sophisticated christological discussions, the issues are not just technical points in theology: they are basic issues that involve the meaning of the gospel.

At times churches have found it necessary to declare a particular interpretation of Christian faith and life to be unfaithful, inappropriate, and a distortion of the gospel. A "heresy" is the church's judgment that a particular interpretation of Christian faith is only a partial truth or that it is a distortion of the truth of the gospel. Such negative judgments are just as tentative and provisional as the church's positive affirmations in its creeds and statements of faith. Both judgments should always be open to subsequent revision and correction. Yesterday's heresies have a way of becoming today's orthodoxies, and vice versa. But because of the negative connotations carried by the term "heresy," it is also important to observe that practically every heretic in the history of Christianity has been *partially* correct. Practically every position that the church has labeled heresy has possessed an element of what Christians believe to be true. Often a position becomes heresy because it tries to build the entire edifice of faith upon only a partial truth, even though what is neglected or omitted is necessary in order to understand the whole truth of the gospel.

Some Christians react cautiously and fearfully to the suggestion that the church may need something more than just the Bible and its ancient creeds in order to articulate its faith. Though caution in these matters is commendable, fear is not helpful. There is wisdom, tried by history, in the church's early creeds. Every attempt at proclamation of the good news in Jesus Christ involves interpretation; one thing to be learned from the early church is that some interpretations are better than others. On the other hand, it is not sufficient simply to repeat what the early church affirmed because a faith that clings to the past and lives in fear of the future cannot be faithful to the God who promises, "See, I am making all things new" (Revelation 21:5). But before we make any judgments about the adequacy of what the early church said about Jesus and before we raise questions about what new directions might be pursued today in Christology, we must first review the church's early creeds.

What Did the Early Church Believe about Jesus?

Almost from the beginning, the church's thinking about Jesus was cast between two ends of a spectrum. At one end was something called Docetism, and at the opposite end was a position known as Ebionism. The church rejected both of these interpretations, declared them to be heresy, and tried to develop its own interpretation of Jesus somewhere between them.

The Ebionites were second-century Jewish Christians who acknowledged Jesus to be the Messiah, but who insisted that he was only a fully human being and not the incarnate Word of God. We may surmise that one reason why the Ebionites refused to confess the deity of Jesus is that their Jewish heritage would not allow them to affirm that Yahweh could be identified with a human being. Jewish Christians continued to confess that "the LORD is our God, the LORD alone" (Deuteronomy 6:4), and any claim that Jesus of Nazareth was the very reality of God would have seemed to contradict that claim. How could Jewish Christians affirm that God alone is Lord and at the same time confess that Jesus is Lord?

The other position was Docetism. The Docetists believed that Jesus of Nazareth was indeed God in the flesh, but that he was not really human. His humanity was only an appearance: he was actually God in disguise. Because the Docetists believed that Jesus was God and that deity by its very nature is unchangeable and impassible, not susceptible to suffering, what the New Testament describes as the agony of Jesus in Gethsemane and on Golgotha's cross was only apparent and not real. Jesus was God in the form of a human being, but not actually a human being.

The church eventually rejected the Docetists' interpretation of Jesus for the same reason it rejected that of the Ebionites. While the latter denied that Jesus was anything other than fully human, the former denied that Jesus was anything other than fully God. Both interpretations threatened the central Christian claim that salvation is God's activity of reconciliation, an activity that has become visible and tangible in Jesus of Nazareth. By denying that in him we encounter the very reality of God, the Ebionites could not say that Jesus is *God's* forgiveness and *God's* act of salvation. What the world encounters in Jesus Christ may be a noble, admirable example of human love and compassion, but not God's love and God's mercy. The Docetists, on the other hand, refused to acknowledge the full humanity of Jesus, and in so doing they were unable to affirm that God's forgiveness and God's salvation had become a reality in the midst of human history, in one who was like all other human beings except that he and he alone was not estranged from the one he called "Father" and from other human beings.

The early church rejected both Ebionism and Docetism as valid interpretations of the gospel. Yet these two positions have never completely disappeared. Even today it is possible to find varieties of each in almost every congregation. Given what we have said about the centrality of Jesus Christ, it is hardly surprising that a docetic or an Ebionite Christology would seriously influence how someone understands and lives Christian faith. Those who affirm that Jesus was a man of unusual moral character, a great teacher and spiritual leader, the primary example of God's kingdom of love and justice in the service of others, but nothing more than that—such people often hold a contemporary version of Ebionism. Jesus is depicted as a powerful moral and spiritual leader, but what Jesus teaches is more important than Jesus himself. Jesus becomes one of many other powerful human examples of compassion and spiritual wisdom. The Sermon on the Mount (and other texts like it) becomes the center of the gospel, and the cross becomes nothing more than the tragic fate of yet another good teacher who came to a bad end.

On the other hand, any interpretation of Jesus that denies his full humanity is a form of Docetism and threatens the Christian understanding of salvation, no less than does Ebionism. Many Christians today deny Jesus his humanity by insisting that he was omniscient and omnipotent. To be human is to exist within the limits of space and time, but docetic interpretations of Jesus insist that he was not confined to his culture and historical location as are all other human beings. They argue that unlike everyone else in first-century Palestine, Jesus knew higher mathematics, modern physics, and the results of recent scientific discoveries. His uncertainty about the future (the day of the coming of the Son of Man) in Mark 13:32 was only a ruse: he knew precisely what the future held for himself and for everyone else. The Docetists' Jesus is the world's greatest magician, capable of altering the probable laws of nature and of performing stunts unmatched even in Hollywood. According to the New Testament, Jesus healed the sick, raised the dead, and cast out demons. Although Jesus' miracles evoke awe and wonder from those who observed them, they are not the basis for the New Testament's confession that Jesus is Lord. Although they were an important part of Jesus' ministry, they are not the foundation of Christian faith. These and other stories in the New Testament that attribute superhuman powers to Jesus must be understood in the context of the early church's faith. They point to Jesus' uniqueness and unrivaled authority and to the kingdom of God, which has drawn near in the person and ministry of Jesus. Both demons ("He commands even the unclean spirits, and they obey him" [Mark 1:27]) and the elemental forces of nature ("What sort of man is this, that even the winds and the sea obey him?" [Matthew 8:27]) submit to him. But these texts should not become the basis for claims that Jesus was either more or less than human.

In the church today, Docetism is probably more widespread than Ebionitism, although the latter often flourishes in college and university religion departments and in New Age spirituality. The church has recognized that both views distort its understanding of the good news that Jesus is God's Word made flesh.

Although the early church rejected Ebionism and Docetism, it took much longer for it to settle on the language it would use to make its confession about Jesus' identity. In the fourth and fifth centuries, the church held a series of councils to resolve the question of what language it would use to interpret its confession that Jesus is Lord. Two of these "ecumenical" councils (councils of the whole household of faith) were especially important—the first at Nicaea in 325 and the fourth at Chalcedon in 451.

At the Council of Nicaea the theological issue was not the relation between humanity and deity in the person of Jesus, but the relation of the first and second persons of the Trinity. Using the language of John's Gospel, many early Christians believed that Jesus was the Word made flesh, the incarnation of the Word, but that still left unresolved the question of the precise nature of the relation between the Word that was incarnate in Jesus and the one whom Jesus called Abba, Father. The first verse of John's Gospel says, "In the beginning was the Word, and the Word was with God, and the Word was God." John's prologue also declares that this same Word "became flesh and lived among us" (1:14).

But what is the relation of this Word that is "full of grace and truth" (1:14) to the first person of the Trinity? It was this question that precipitated the Council of Nicaea.

This was a pivotal moment for the early church, but the significance of that debate over the status of the Word in relation to the Father was not confined to the life of the early church. It remains a major issue today. Without the doctrine of the Trinity, important issues in Christology remain confused and unresolved. An example of the importance of the Trinity and the significance of the Council of Nicaea for understanding Jesus' identity was a furor that took place several years ago in the Presbyterian Church. A minister from another denomination received a call to be the copastor of a Presbyterian congregation. When he was examined in that presbytery, he was asked whether he could affirm that Jesus is God. He responded, "Only God is God." That answer precipitated a lively debate, one in which there was considerably more emotional heat than theological insight. The Council of Nicaea is directly relevant to that controversy.

The minister's response was both right and wrong. He was correct in that the New Testament does not say that Jesus and the one he calls Father are the same person. When Jesus prays in Gethsemane to one he calls Father and teaches his disciples to do the same, he is not praying to himself. When Jesus says in John's Gospel, "The Father and I are one" (10:30), he is not claiming that he is the Father. The Word made flesh in Jesus of Nazareth is a reality, a "person," distinct from the first and third persons of the Trinity: the Father and the Spirit. Matthew's Gospel affirms that Jesus' name was Emmanuel, "God is with us" (1:23), but during Jesus' ministry the heavens were not empty. Jesus continues to pray to his Father and to proclaim his Father's kingdom. According to the apostle Paul, "in Christ God was reconciling the world to himself" (2 Corinthians 5:19), and the preposition "in" is terribly important in Christian theology. There is an identity of sorts between the Father, Word/Son, and Spirit, but there is distinction as well.

Many Christians today are no less confused about this important issue than were Christians in the early church. In part the confusion is rooted in the Bible. Jesus repeatedly refers to the one to whom he prays as "Abba/Father." So too do the apostle Paul and the other writers of the New Testament. But Paul also appears to use the terms "Father" and "God" synonymously, as though they refer to the same reality. For example, the final verse of Paul's Second Letter to the Christians in Corinth is often used as a benediction in Christian worship services. "The grace of the Lord Jesus Christ, the love of God, and the communion of the Holy Spirit be with all of you" (13:13). This verse appears to be "Trinitarian," but if it is read as a description of the Trinity, then it suggests that "God" is the name of the first person of the Trinity, that God and Father are therefore synonymous, and that "our Lord Jesus Christ" and "the Holy Spirit" are not God, but somehow subordinate to God or lesser gods. It was precisely this interpretation that Nicaea denied. What Nicaea (and later Constantinople in 381) affirmed is that the three distinct but inseparable persons—Father, Son, and Holy Spirit—are one reality, one God, and that "God" in Christian faith is not the name of the first person of the Trinity but the name of these three persons in their one divine life and their relation to one another. The Word and the Spirit are no less (and no more) "God" than is the Father.

The doctrine of the Trinity, developed at Nicaea in 325 (and at Constantinople in 381), was the church's attempt to clarify the "grammar" of Christian faith—how it speaks about and understands the reality of God as that which has been disclosed to it in Jesus Christ, in the Bible, and in its worship and experience. The Trinity clarifies the sense in which Jesus is and is not God. Without the Trinity, the Christian confession that the Word made flesh in Jesus of Nazareth and the Father are one becomes hopelessly confusing. Unfortunately, what happened at Nicaea and what the church means by its confession that God is triune are rarely discussed in most congregations.

At Nicaea the major theological issue was the relation between the Son, or the Word who is incarnate in Jesus, and the one Jesus refers to as Abba, or Father (Matthew 6:9; Mark 14:36; Luke 23:34, 46; John 17). Was only the Father to be called "God," or were the Father and the Son (or the Word) and the Spirit what is meant by "God"? But if all three are God, how is Christian faith not a form of polytheism (a belief in more than one god)?

Two different positions emerged in the early fourth century in the Egyptian city of Alexandria. On one side was a man named Arius, and on the other side were Alexander and Athanasius. Arius and his followers argued that God, who is holy and transcendent, could not be divisible. Because of God's majesty and uniqueness, it was inconceivable to the Arians that the Son or Word could be identified with God. The Arian position came to be identified with a theological slogan: "There was a time when the Son was not." For Arius and his followers, in other words, there was a fundamental distinction between God the Father and the Son. In the great divide between God and creation, the Son was the apex of creation, but on the creaturely side of the divide. On the other hand, the Christians in Alexandria who identified with Alexander and Athanasius considered Arius's understanding of the Son or Word to be wholly unacceptable and a threat to their understanding of Jesus as Savior. Alexander and Athanasius believed that it was precisely because the Son, who is truly God and assumed real human flesh, that salvation is a reality in human history and human beings are no longer enslaved by sin. The Son and the Father are distinct, but they are of the same substance or essence.

The Nicene Council sided with Alexander (who died the following year) and Athanasius against Arius; the council rejected the basic tenets of what came to be known as "Arianism" by denying that the Son was created and by insisting that he was "begotten" by the Father before all creation. By "begotten" Nicaea did not mean that the Father created the Son or caused the Son to come into existence, but that the Son is to be understood in his relation to the Father; that is, the Son is the one sent by the Father. Furthermore, Nicaea affirmed that the Son is of the same substance or reality as the Father (the technical term is *homoousios*) and consequently has the same attributes as the Father. Father and Son differ only in the way they are related to one another.

Why does this debate matter? If one knows nothing of Arius, Alexander, and Athanasius and the issues they debated, then it is possible to misread the Nicene Creed. It clearly affirms the divinity of the Son or Word who was incarnate in Jesus of Nazareth. It does so because what was in question as a result of Arius's theology was the Son's divinity. No one, except Docetists, doubted that Jesus of Nazareth was a first-century human being. However, the reader today who perhaps knows little or nothing about the Nicene Creed might conclude that the early church affirmed only the deity of Jesus Christ and either denied or ignored his humanity. Given the widespread Docetism in the church today, there are good grounds for suspecting that many Christians have come to that conclusion. Only if one knows the history of the Nicene Creed will it be clear that early fourth-century Christians had no intention of affirming Jesus' deity at the expense of his humanity.

When the minister referred to above answered the question as to whether Jesus is God by saying "Only God is God," he re-created the issues that led to the Nicene Creed. Yes, only God is God, but the minister appeared to be denying that Jesus is God. Jesus is not the first person of the Trinity (or Father), but in Christian faith Jesus Christ, the Word incarnate, and the Holy Spirit are no less God than is the first person of the Trinity (or the one whom Jesus addresses as Father).

The Council of Nicaea, however, did not answer all questions about the identity of Jesus Christ. It only stirred up more questions. Although Nicaea affirmed that the Son or Word who is incarnate in Jesus of Nazareth is of the very reality of God, it did not resolve the question of Jesus' humanity and deity. In the fourth century two major schools of thought about Jesus' identity emerged. One was centered around Antioch and the other around Alexandria (which with Jerusalem and Rome were the four major centers of early Christianity). The latter, the Alexandrian school, which had been the home of Alexander and Athanasius, focused on the incarnation and emphasized that Jesus Christ is the Word of God made flesh. One of the best-known treatises of the fourth century is Athanasius's *On the Incarnation of the Word*. The Alexandrian school is sometimes described as a Word/flesh Christology, and its best-known representative is Cyril of Alexandria (ca. 378–444). Critics of this school worried that while it clearly affirmed Jesus' deity by emphasizing that he is God's Word made flesh, it seemed to them that it failed to affirm his full humanity. There is more to being human than just the flesh.

One member of the Alexandrian school, a man named Apollinaris of Laodicea (d. 390), argued that Paul's claim in 2 Corinthians 5:19 that the Word was "in" Christ meant that it had taken the place of Jesus' rational mind or soul. In a way this interpretation makes good sense. It explains many New Testament passages in which Jesus seems to have an uncommon wisdom and to know more than other people do. However, if the Word replaced Jesus' rational mind, then Jesus was certainly either more or less than human. In any case such an interpretation seemed to deny Jesus' full humanity. Was Apollinaris simply making explicit the necessary implication of the Alexandrian position, or had he distorted it, turning it into a form of Docetism?

The interpretation of Jesus' identity that emerged from Antioch and from theologians such as Diodore of Tarsus (d. 390) and Theodore of Mopsuestia (350–428) has been described as a Word/man Christology (in distinction from the Alexandrian Word/flesh Christology). The Antiochenes were troubled by the way in which the Alexandrians seemed to compromise Jesus' full humanity and insisted that Jesus was both fully human and fully God. They sought to protect Jesus' full humanity by insisting that Jesus, like all human beings, grew and developed in his knowledge of the world and his understanding of it. They did not deny his deity, but they resisted any interpretation of Jesus' identity seeming to deny that he was fully and truly human. The issue came to a head when Nestorius (ca. 386–451) refused to describe Mary as "mother of God" (Theotokos) and referred to her as "mother of Christ." Theotokos sounded to Nestorius like another Alexandrian affirmation of Jesus' divinity at the expense of his humanity. However, the Antiochenes' emphasis on the distinctiveness of Jesus' two natures, his deity and humanity, worried the Alexandrians. They were concerned that in the Antiochene description of Jesus, distinction became separation, and if Jesus' two natures were separated, then the claim that Jesus is one person became unintelligible.

At a series of councils and synods in the fourth century, the two sides took turns in discovering extreme positions in the other camp that could be denounced as heresy. The Antiochenes accused the Alexandrians of denying Jesus' humanity and lapsing into Docetism; the Alexandrians accused the Antiochenes of separating the two natures and denying the unity of Jesus' person. The differences were at least partly semantic. That is, the two schools were using different theological terms in their interpretations of Jesus' identity, and the terms they shared seemed to mean something different in each school. At two fifth-century councils—Ephesus in 431 (the third ecumenical council) and Chalcedon in 451 (the fourth ecumenical council)—the larger church was finally able to reach agreement on language and a formula to describe the person of Christ. The Chalcedonian formula became the church's normative interpretation of Jesus Christ. It affirmed both that Jesus was indeed one person (satisfying the Alexandrians) in two distinct (satisfying the Antiochenes) but inseparable natures, fully human and fully God:

> the same perfect in Godhead, the same perfect in manhood, truly God and truly man, the same of a reasonable soul and body; consubstantial with the Father in Godhead, and the same consubstantial with us in manhood, like us in all things except sin, . . . acknowledged in two natures without confusion, without change, without division, without separation.[2]

This Chalcedonian formula acknowledged the Antiochene concern that Jesus' full humanity be affirmed. It affirmed the distinctiveness of both natures in Jesus without confusion or separation. And it acknowledged the Alexandrian concern that Jesus' natures not be separated, that he is indeed one person, not two persons rattling around in one human body. Jesus Christ is both true and authentic humanity and the full reality of God with us.

Chalcedon did not, however, settle the matter of Jesus' identity. The belief that Jesus is truly God and of only one nature developed into what came to be known as Monophysitism (literally, "one nature"), and both it and its counterpoint, Nestorianism, continued to find adherents in the ancient church after Chalcedon. The Chacedonian Decree did become and has remained the normative interpretation of Jesus' identity for most Christian churches. For Christian faith the two fundamental claims made by Nicaea and Chalcedon are that the Son or Word incarnate in Jesus of Nazareth is of the same substance or reality as the Father, and that Jesus of Nazareth is himself both fully human and fully God, two natures in one person.

A common reaction to the early church's discussions of Christ is a suspicion that the church's theologians may have done more harm than good by means of their technical formulas and their attempts to distinguish between distinct but inseparable natures. Though such suspicions are understandable, they are also unfortunate because those gathered at Nicaea, Constantinople, Ephesus, and Chalcedon were acutely aware that they were trying to say something that for the sake of the gospel and the world had to be said because it is good news about God's redemption of a sinful world. They also knew that it is something that no words and no formula can ever adequately express because at the heart of it all is a holy mystery that finally transcends human comprehension. Though no words, no formula, can ever be fully adequate, they recognized that if the church intended to be faithful to its commission to proclaim the gospel (Matthew 28:18–20), it must make its confession about Jesus Christ as clear and as intelligible as possible.

Just as Chalcedon did not bring the debates about Jesus' identity to a close in the fifth century, so too numerous questions have continued to be raised inside and outside the church about these ancient formulas. Some people today find these questions and criticisms compelling and believe that for the sake of the gospel the church must develop new language and new paradigms to interpret its confession that "God was in Christ." Yet it must be remembered that the church has not clung to those ancient formulas simply out of stubbornness. It has continued to use those formulas as benchmarks by which it measures all other attempts to say who Jesus is because thus far none of the others has seemed to come as close to the heart of the Christian mystery. As G. K. Chesterton (1874–1936) wrote many years ago:

> For orthodox theology has specifically insisted that Christ was not a being apart from God and man, like an elf, nor yet a being half human and half not, like a centaur, but both things at once and both things thoroughly, very man and very God.[3]

That is the holy mystery that Christians believe about Jesus Christ, and no human formula has or ever will quite exhaust its depths. The Danish theologian Søren Kierkegaard (1813–55) made the same point. "At every moment Christ is God just as much as he is man—just as the sky seems to be as deep in the sea as it is high above the sea."[4]

Why Do Some Christians Now Find Classical Christology Inadequate?

For many centuries the Nicene Creed and the Chalcedonian Council's descriptions of Jesus Christ were widely accepted. During the sixteenth century, Martin Luther, John Calvin, and many other leaders of the Protestant Reformation readily affirmed the Christology developed in the fourth and fifth centuries. But during the European Enlightenment of the seventeenth and eighteenth centuries, questions were raised about the authoritative status of the Bible and the authoritative role of tradition and creeds in Christian faith. Those questions in turn prompted others about the adequacy of classical Christology. As we will see in chapter 5, those questions led to various proposals in the nineteenth and twentieth centuries about how to reinterpret Jesus' identity in ways more congenial to a post-Enlightenment world.

Of the many questions that have been raised about classical Christology, three are particularly important. The first concerns the intelligibility of its language, the second its neglect of Jesus' ministry, and the third asks whether sufficient attention has been given to Jesus' humanity.

First, many theologians have asked whether the classical view of Christ is intelligible in a time and culture far removed from that of fourth- and fifth-century Christianity. As we have observed, no creed or confession is timeless and adequate for every age and culture. Every creed, including the so-called ecumenical creeds of the early church, addresses particular questions that have arisen at a specific point in history. A creed is successful if it addresses those questions in language that is both clear and intelligible on the one hand, and on the other hand faithfully reflects the witness of the Bible and the convictions of the early church. Understandably, classical Christology used terms borrowed from Greek and Roman culture in the fourth and fifth centuries, terms such as "substance," "essence," and "nature," but these terms may no longer be intelligible to Christians living in the twenty-first century. They simply no longer mean the same thing they did to the people who wrote and recited them in the early church. If it were possible to survey Christians today in North America or Nigeria or South Korea who continue to use the Nicene Creed in their worship services, we might well discover that few understand what is meant by the claim that Jesus Christ is "of one substance with the Father." Indeed, if Christians today were pressed to explain what they think those words mean, we may discover that Arius won the debate at Nicaea, not Alexander and Athanasius.

Part of the problem is that we no longer understand anthropology or what it means to be human the same way people did in the fourth and fifth centuries. Terms such as "substance" and "nature" were familiar and appropriate then, but they no longer reflect our understandings of humanity. Our interpretations of the human today are shaped not as much by Plato and Aristotle as they are by the social sciences, such as psychology, cultural anthropology, and sociology, disciplines unknown to the early church. Consequently, Christians today cannot describe the identity of Jesus in categories such as substance and nature without running the high risk of being seriously misunderstood or simply ignored. That does not mean that Nicaea and Chalcedon should be discarded. They have served and will continue to serve as benchmarks, as guides and instructors for contemporary Christians, but by themselves they are no longer sufficient as interpretations of Jesus' identity as the Christ. Contemporary Christians must develop new language and paradigms to clarify their confession that Jesus is the Christ and that in him God has reconciled and will reconcile all people and all things. As we shall see in the next chapter, much of the Christology that has been written in the nineteenth and twentieth centuries has been devoted to the difficult task of developing that new language.

Second, in addition to the problem of reinterpreting classical Christology, many theologians have been troubled by the focus in Nicaea and Chalcedon on Jesus' birth, death, and resurrection and by their neglect of his life and ministry. In both the Nicene Creed and the Chalcedonian Decree, the emphasis falls heavily on the incarnation, the claim in John's Gospel that Jesus of Nazareth is the Word made flesh. Yet in either creed, very little is said about the rest of Jesus' life. His teaching about the kingdom of God, his exorcisms, and his healing miracles are not mentioned. Mark's summary statement about Jesus at the beginning of his Gospel—that he came proclaiming "'The time is fulfilled, and the kingdom of God has come near; repent, and believe in the good news'" (1:15)—is not acknowledged at Nicaea or Chalcedon. The writers of those early creeds were surely familiar with the stories in the Gospels, but if our knowledge of Jesus and Christian faith were restricted to the creeds of the fourth and fifth centuries, we would have no idea that the central theme in Jesus' ministry was the kingdom of God. Given the questions and issues that confronted the early church, it is hardly surprising that they focused on the incarnation, but many Christians today worry about the implications of the early church's neglect of Jesus' ministry.

We understand a person's identity not simply in terms of what they look like and what kind of person they are or what their character is, but also in terms of what they do—their behavior—and how they respond to others and the events that make up their lives. Jesus of Nazareth is no different. That Mary was his mother and that he grew up in Nazareth tell us important things about him, but his character and identity are more evident in his actions and in the life he lives, stories that make up the bulk of the material in the Gospels. Neither the infancy stories in Matthew and Luke nor the different accounts of his death and resurrection in the Gospels provide a basis for the church's claim that Jesus was like all other human beings "yet without sin" (Hebrews 4:15). That claim is best understood in terms of the Gospels' descriptions of how Jesus lived his life.

One way to understand human sin is that it reflects the incoherence between what a person says and does. The New Testament describes sinful humans as "liars" not simply because they fail to speak truthfully, but in the far more significant sense that what they say does not finally cohere with what they do, with the way they live. Jesus, on the other hand, is "sinless" because what he does, the way he lives his life, perfectly coheres with what he says. Not only does Jesus teach that one should love God with all one's heart, but Jesus also lives that way. Not only does Jesus teach that one should love one's neighbors, but Jesus also lives that way. Not only does Jesus teach that one should forgive one's enemies, but Jesus also lives that way. As Jesus dies on the cross, he prays, "Father, forgive them; for they do not know what they are doing" (Luke 23:34). There is no incoherence, no degree of separation, between what Jesus does and the way he lives his life. One would not know that, however, if Christian faith were simply a description of Jesus' birth, death, and resurrection. It is his life and ministry, as described in the Gospels, that enables Christians to understand the claim that he is "the Word made flesh" and "God with us."

Furthermore, the ministry of Jesus is vitally important for many Christians today who are struggling to understand what discipleship and mission mean in the twenty-first century. What does it mean for individuals and communities to "follow" Jesus in the new world of the twenty-first century? Early Christians were sometimes described as "people of the way," and "the way" was understood to be the life lived by Jesus. "I am the way, and the truth, and the life," says Jesus in John's Gospel (14:6). Jesus' way is what he said and did and his interactions with those around him. Although Christians cannot be little Christs, Jesus' long journey from Nazareth to the cross has provided the template for Christian discipleship and mission across the centuries. Following Jesus is not simply a matter of believing the right things about him, or even doing the same things that Jesus did. It is not that simple. According to the New Testament, following Jesus entails turning around in one's life and traveling in a different direction and toward a different goal.

Jesus' ministry is vitally important because it shows Christians where they should go with their lives; it tells them how they should live as they make that journey; and it describes what kind of people they will become if they choose to live that way.

In addition to the concern about the intelligibility of the church's early creeds and their neglect of Jesus' ministry, a third reason why contemporary theologians find classical Christology inadequate is that it seems to make Jesus' deity more important than his humanity. To be sure, Nicaea insists not only that Jesus was conceived by the Holy Spirit, as is no other human being, but also that he was born of Mary: in claiming that he was born of a woman, as are all human beings, it thus affirms his full humanity. Nevertheless, by emphasizing Jesus' birth and then jumping directly to his death and resurrection, the early creeds seem to imply that the human life Jesus lived is of no consequence for understanding his identity. John Calvin seems to say as much in the catechism he wrote for Christians in Geneva. In his exposition of the Apostles' Creed, Calvin has the child ask (Question 55), "Why do you go immediately from His [Christ's] birth to His death, passing over the whole history of His life?" And Calvin has the minister respond: "Because nothing is said here about what belongs properly to the substance of our redemption."[5] If the life Jesus lived has nothing to do with the meaning of redemption, one can understand why some Christians over the centuries may have had the impression that Jesus' humanity was either of lesser importance in relation to his deity or of no significance whatsoever.

When the early creeds are interpreted in their historical contexts, their emphasis on incarnation, cross, and resurrection is understandable. But when they are read apart from those contexts, they can and have been read as affirming Jesus' deity and ignoring or even denying his humanity: his teaching, exorcisms, and ministry. The consequence of such a deemphasis or denial of Jesus' humanity is a Christology that threatens to become a form of Docetism. That kind of misinterpretation might not occur if careful attention is given to the Gospels in the New Testament, which do not "go immediately" from birth to resurrection. On the contrary, they linger over important events in Jesus' teaching and ministry as if they are trying to tell us that neither Jesus' birth nor his death and resurrection can be understood apart from the entire story of the Jesus who has proclaimed God's kingdom and enacted it in his eating and drinking with the outcasts of society, as though the last were already first and the first last.

Twentieth-century confessions emphasize both the importance of Jesus' ministry and the significance of his humanity. Both The Confession of 1967 and A Brief Statement of Faith (1991) of the Presbyterian Church (U.S.A.) give a more prominent place to Jesus' ministry than do the church's early creeds and those of the Reformation. The Confession of 1967 (C-67) emphasizes 2 Corinthians 5:16–21 and God's reconciliation in Jesus Christ in order to address what discipleship and mission mean for a church in North America facing social issues of racism, war, poverty, and gender discrimination. But before discussing what reconciliation means for these specific issues, C-67 declares that in Jesus "true humanity was realized once for all."[6] Thus C-67 recognizes that for Christian faith, reconciliation is not an abstraction but something that has a particular shape in the life of Jesus of Nazareth. What reconciliation means for complicated issues such as racism, war, poverty, and sexuality can be discerned only by looking first at reconciliation as it is embodied in Jesus of Nazareth.

In the 1970s the Presbyterian Church in the United States considered a contemporary confession titled A Declaration of Faith. Like The Confession of 1967, it places greater emphasis on the humanity of Jesus than do some of the classical confessions:

> Jesus was what we are,
> He grew up in a family and a society
> troubled by the common problems of the world.
> His knowledge was limited
> by his time and place in history.
> He felt deeply the joy of friendship
> and the hurt of being rejected.

Jesus prayed,
struggled with temptation,
knew anger,
and was subject to suffering and death.
He was like us in every way except sin.[7]

This Declaration of Faith emphasizes Jesus' healing and teaching, and it links the mission of the church to Jesus' ministry. At the same time it does not ignore the central claims of the classical creeds. It stands in the same tradition as Nicaea and Chalcedon when it affirms that in Jesus of Nazareth the world encounters the reality of God:

In the person and work of Jesus,
God himself and a human life
are united but not confused,
distinguished but not separated.
The coming of Jesus was itself
the coming of God's promised rule.
Through his birth, death, and resurrection
he brings about the relationship between God and humanity
that God always intended.[8]

Chapter Five

What Are People Today Saying about Jesus?

What Are Theologians Today Saying about Jesus?

For the past two hundred years, theologians have tried to find language that would enable the church to confess its faith in Jesus Christ in a way that would be intelligible both to those in the church who are not professional theologians and to non-Christians in the larger culture. Most theologians engaged in this task have not rejected the interpretation of Jesus in the church's classical creeds and confessions. They have continued to be guided and instructed by that confessional heritage and have tried to avoid the mistakes and pitfalls that the early church rejected. With their predecessors in the ancient church, modern theologians share a common confession that Jesus Christ is Lord, but they also recognize, as did their predecessors, the importance of making the church's faith in Jesus Christ understandable and compelling for contemporary society. Consequently, they have tried to develop language and imagery that is consistent with the witness of the church through the ages but also speaks clearly and meaningfully to contemporary culture.

The attempt to find appropriate and adequate language to confess faith in Jesus is not just a matter of translation. The challenge is not as easy as simply developing new language for the purpose of translating ancient creeds. In proposing new language for the church to confess its faith in Jesus Christ, theologians have also altered the meaning of traditional doctrines about the "person" and "work" of Jesus. In most cases their new proposals for how to understand Jesus reflect contemporary experiences of God's grace and therein the meaning of the gospel. In this chapter we will briefly survey a few of the many proposals that have been made by contemporary theologians for reinterpreting Christology.

Almost every new proposal for how to understand Christian faith during the last two hundred years has included a reinterpretation of Christology. Because Jesus Christ is the center of Christian faith, as we noted in chapter 1, reinterpretations of Christian faith often have begun with a rethinking of the church's understanding of Jesus' identity as the Christ. A history of theology in the nineteenth and twentieth centuries could easily be written as a study of theologians' many attempts to reinterpret Jesus' identity and significance. Here it is not possible to discuss all of them or even most of them, but five basic types are prominent in contemporary discussion: (1) Jesus as a person of perfect God-consciousness; (2) Jesus as mediator of the experience of salvation; (3) Jesus as liberator; (4) Jesus as the basis for eschatological hope; and (5) Jesus as the embodiment of wisdom. By no means are these the only reconstructions of Christology that have been proposed. There are many others, but these are prominent examples of some of the issues that have concerned theologians. In addition to these five types of Christology, we will conclude this chapter by examining recent proposals in narrative Christology. In chapter 6 we will turn to some of the new proposals in Christology from theologians in the non-Western world and to a discussion of Jesus Christ in relation to the world's other religions.

What Is Jesus' Perfect God-Consciousness?

The first major proposal for the reinterpretation of Christology in the modern period, and still one of the most important, was that by Friedrich Schleiermacher (1768–1834) in *The Christian Faith* (published in 1821–22 and revised in 1830–31). He departed from the categories of classical Christology—one person in two natures—and interpreted Jesus' identity in terms of his perfect God-consciousness.[1] In so doing he was reacting against not only classical metaphysics, but also the emphasis on reason and morality that had dominated the European Enlightenment of the seventeenth and eighteenth centuries. He reflects the rediscovery of the affective dimension of human existence that had recently emerged in European Romanticism.

As Schleiermacher interprets him, Jesus is the mediator of the experience of redemption in the Christian community. He is mediator because his "sensible consciousness" is determined at every moment by a perfect God-consciousness, an awareness of God unlike that of all other human beings, whose God-consciousness is distorted by human sin. Jesus' perfect God-consciousness was not a static reality, as the two natures appeared to be in classical Christology, but grew and developed in ways that were always appropriate to Jesus' age and maturity. It was his perfect God-consciousness that made Jesus unique and differentiated him from the rest of humanity, whose lives are marred by sin—which Schleiermacher described as "God-forgetfulness" and by which he meant not a trivial lapse of memory, but living in the world as though God were not. Jesus redeems a sinful world by means of his continuing presence and activity in the life of the church.

Schleiermacher's use of the idiom of "God-consciousness" left a lasting impression on nineteenth- and twentieth-century Christology and New Testament studies. Throughout the modern period there have been many attempts to describe Jesus' self-consciousness. How did Jesus understand himself? Did he believe he was the Son of God? Is that how we should interpret the so-called messianic secret (Jesus' repeated commands to those around him that they not disclose his true identity)? Much of this new way of thinking about Jesus was inspired, directly or indirectly, by Schleiermacher. Many theologians and biblical scholars have concluded, perhaps mistakenly, that if they could only determine how Jesus understood himself, they would have a clue as to what it means to name him the Christ and what the apostle Paul meant when he wrote that God was "in him."

Schleiermacher by no means was the only theologian to use the idiom of God-consciousness to describe Jesus. A hundred and fifty years later a debate occurred in England in both academic circles and the popular press concerning the meaning of the incarnation. Using ideas borrowed directly from Schleiermacher, one of the best-known participants, John Hick, argued that what was distinctive and significant about Jesus was the intensity of his consciousness of God. Jesus was so acutely attuned to God that he could speak of God with remarkable authority[2] (in the next chapter we will return to Hick's Christology).

There are several advantages to the use of the term "God-consciousness" to describe Jesus' relation to the one he called Father. First, the term strongly affirms the humanity of Jesus. Christologies that begin with Jesus' perfect God-consciousness are not driven to the unfortunate position of dividing Jesus into two natures, with all the problems that the language of "two natures" created for classical Christology. Schleiermacher begins with Jesus' human consciousness and argues that his "uniqueness" was that his consciousness was determined wholly by his sense of the presence and reality of God. Second, as a description of human identity, the term "consciousness" is more familiar and intelligible to contemporary people than the categories of "nature" and "substance." It is more compatible with a modern understanding of human identity that is dynamic, developmental, and psychological. It is not something that is fixed and unchanging, but something that grows and develops. If Jesus of Nazareth was indeed "fully human" (to use the classical language), then he too must have grown and developed—not just physically but also in his self-understanding and in his relation to the one he addressed as Abba, Father.

But there are also serious problems with Christologies that appeal to Jesus' God-consciousness in either their nineteenth-century or late twentieth-century forms. One problem is that New Testament scholarship has demonstrated the difficulty, if not the impossibility, of determining precisely how Jesus understood himself and his relation to his Father. As we stated in chapter 2, the Gospels are not biographies but proclamations of

Easter faith, and as such they do not give the reader access to the historical Jesus' intentions, motives, and self-understanding, or his understanding of his relation to God.

Furthermore, it is not evident that the appeal to Jesus' God-consciousness is an improvement on the interpretation of Jesus' identity in the ancient creeds. The interpretations of Jesus by Schleiermacher and Hick may be only modern versions of Ebionism: interpretations that affirm Jesus' humanity and enable us to understand him the way we do other human beings, but that are not adequate to convey the New Testament's claim that he is "God with us" (Matthew 1:23). The early church clearly wanted to say something more about Jesus than that his consciousness of God was "perfect" or undistorted by sin. The classical creeds affirm that in his person and acts, Jesus was the very embodiment of the reality of God. Jesus was not simply acutely aware of the presence of God: in his person and activity he was the reality of God's grace and love in the world. Additionally, Christologies that appeal to Jesus' God-consciousness have not been any more successful than their classical predecessors in making sense out of what the early church described as "the hypostatic union"—the union of the human and divine natures in the one person Jesus of Nazareth. Neither Schleiermacher nor Hick has given a compelling interpretation of Jesus' perfect God-consciousness that does justice to the early church's conviction that the man Jesus is not only human but also "fully God."

How Have Theologians Reinterpreted Redemption?

A second proposal in contemporary Christology makes Jesus Christ the mediator of or occasion for the experience of redemption. This type of Christology has appeared in various forms during the past two hundred years, but most versions of it have in common an emphasis on the experience of redemption as the basis for the church's confession that God was in Christ. Schleiermacher laid the foundation for this proposal by describing the New Testament picture of Jesus as a reflection of the early church's experience of redemption. In many versions of this form of Christology, the emphasis falls more on the church's experience of redemption than it does on the figure of the historical Jesus.

In the nineteenth century this interpretation was proposed by Albrecht Ritschl (1822–89), who described Jesus of Nazareth as uniquely conscious of a new relation to God that was expressed in the primary symbol of the kingdom of God.[3] Both Jesus' disciples and subsequent Christian communities experience the meaning and reality of that kingdom when they imitate Jesus and are conformed to him, who is the prototype of humanity's spiritual vocation. It is the Christian community's experience of redemption through Jesus that gives rise to the claim that God was in him.

Two quite different types of this form of Christology are those of the German Lutheran Rudolf Bultmann (1884–1976) and the Dutch Roman Catholic Edward Schillebeeckx (1914–2009). For Bultmann, the basis for Christian faith and theology is the encounter between individuals and the event of the proclamation of God's Word.[4] If people respond in faith and obedience to the preached Word, then they experience an authentic existence: the love and freedom that enable them to live in the world as though they were not of it. In the early church it was this experience of faith in response to the cross that was the basis for the Christian life ("For I decided to know nothing among you except Jesus Christ, and him crucified" [1 Corinthians 2:2]). And in the church today it is this same experience of faith in response to the proclamation of Jesus the crucified Christ that is the basic Christian reality.

In his massive volumes *Jesus* (1974) and *Christ* (1977), Schillebeeckx focuses his attention on Christian experience, but unlike Bultmann he attempts to establish a connection between Jesus' own experience—what he describes as Jesus' "Abba experience"—and the experience in early Christian communities of the continuing and abiding presence of the resurrected Jesus and the expectation of his return.[5]

In each of these proposals, it is Christian experience that is the basis for the church's claim that Jesus is the incarnation of God's Word. This type of Christology has a number of strengths. First, most versions of it recognize that confessional claims about Jesus are closely related to experiences and interpretations of redemption, and consequently, they pay less attention to philosophical questions about the relation of deity and humanity in Jesus than they do to the experience of faith and redemption and the sense in which Jesus of Nazareth mediates that experience. Theologians who take this approach recognize that if discussions about Christology do not illumine the experience of faith, they will be of little or no interest to most Christian people. In addition, they recognize that categories used to interpret Christology that are directly related to experience are still meaningful to many people, while metaphysical and ontological categories are not.

Interpretations of Jesus based on experiences of salvation reflect a number of important developments that have occurred since the European Enlightenment of the seventeenth and eighteenth centuries. Perhaps the most important of these is that the primary criterion for determining the truth of an assertion has become wholly subjective. In the modern age, personal experience has become the primary criterion for determining both the meaning and the truth of any assertion. Christologies of this second type, based on experiences of faith and redemption, reflect that development. That is one reason why many theologians today give scant attention to questions of historicity and metaphysics and focus on personal experience, either that of the theologian or that of a particular group of people. If Christian faith cannot be shown to directly reflect a particular group's experience, it runs the risk of being dismissed as irrelevant.

Although versions of this interpretation of Jesus recognize the inseparability of Christian convictions about Jesus' identity and experiences of him as Savior—what theologians describe as the inseparability of Christology and soteriology—they too have serious difficulties. Two are especially important. First, in shifting the emphasis from the person of Jesus to the Christian experience of redemption, this type of Christology raises questions about the dispensability of the Jesus of history and perhaps even the Christ of Christian faith. If the primary reality of Christian faith is the experience of redemption, then it may be unclear why the figure of Jesus is necessary for the mediation of that experience.

If Jesus is simply an example of that experience or merely the occasion for it, then the experience itself rather than Jesus would seem to be what matters, and the claims of contemporary Christology become something fundamentally different from those of the classical creeds. Second, in this second type of Christology, even if Jesus is in some way necessary for the mediation of redemption, it often appears that it is the experience of redemption that identifies Jesus rather than Jesus identifying the meaning of redemption. In classical Christianity an understanding of Jesus' identity (his "person") is inseparable from the experience of him as Redeemer (what he does or his "work"), but it is Jesus who identifies what Christians mean by terms such as redemption and salvation. In some forms of charismatic Christianity, for example, it often seems that it is a spiritual experience that identifies who Jesus is rather than Jesus who identifies what is and is not an experience of the Spirit of Christ. "Test the spirits," cautions the writer of First John, "to see whether they are from God," and the criterion for that test is whether that spirit "confesses that Jesus Christ has come in the flesh" (4:1–3).

What Is Liberation Christology?

Liberation Christology is a third type of contemporary Christology that has emerged in some African American churches and in Latin America, Korea, and other countries in the so-called two-thirds world. In many ways liberation Christology is similar to the first two types we have examined. There is no single form of liberation Christology, but many versions of it make the experience of oppression (either racial or social) and the hope for liberation the central themes of Christian faith. And in most forms of liberation Christology, Jesus is not so much the Mediator, as he was understood in much of classical Christology, as he is the Liberator, who frees the oppressed and who calls the church to take part in God's triumph over racism, sexism, classism, and colonialism. Jesus comes to liberate not only oppressed peoples' souls but also their "bodies" (both personal and communal). Liberation Christology has developed in churches and communities for whom oppression is a daily reality and not simply an academic topic, for whom God's preferential option for the poor is not simply an interesting idea but also something that sustains daily existence.

Most forms of this third type of Christology emphasize that liberation is not a new idea but an important theme throughout the Bible. Examples abound: God liberates Israel from bondage in Egypt (Exodus 2–14). Through the voices of the prophets, God demands that Israel care for the widow, the orphan, the sojourner, and the poor. Jesus preaches in his hometown that Isaiah's hope that good news will one day be preached to the poor, that captives will one day be released, that the blind will one day be healed, and that the oppressed will one day be set free has now been fulfilled by him (Luke 4:16–21). Jesus teaches that God judges the nations of the earth on the basis of whether they have cared for the "least" of God's children—the hungry, the thirsty, the stranger, the naked, the sick, and the imprisoned (Matthew 25:31–46). Perhaps affluent Christians have failed to notice that God's liberation of the oppressed is a prominent theme in the Bible because it is in their self-interest to do so.

An axiom of liberation theology in general and liberation Christology in particular is that "praxis" (commitment to and solidarity with a particular oppressed community and its struggle for justice) precedes reflection. Liberation Christology begins not with thinking or reflection, not with metaphysical discussions about the person of Jesus, but with following Jesus, with discipleship based on Jesus' life and ministry and his enactment of the kingdom and justice of God. It is not surprising, therefore, that liberation Christology is far more interested in discipleship and what is involved in being a follower of Jesus than it is in the interpretation of the two natures in the one person of Jesus Christ. In other words, liberation theology begins not with reflection about Jesus, but with active discipleship, with the decision to follow and obey him.

Of the many books on liberation Christology, some of the most important are those by the Jesuit theologian Jon Sobrino: *Christology at the Crossroads*, *Jesus the Liberator*, and *Christ the Liberator*.[6] In his first book Sobrino does not devote a single chapter to the theme of liberation; rather, liberation is the single theme that runs through several chapters on the historical Jesus. Like most other liberation theologians, Sobrino believes it is important that Christology begin "from below," from what can be known about the historical Jesus: Jesus' proclamation of the kingdom and what Sobrino refers to as "the faith of Jesus." By focusing on the historical Jesus, one learns the distinctive features of Christian liberation. It is Jesus in his historical particularity that is the basis for Christian faith and discipleship. Like some of the theologians in the first type of Christology, Sobrino thinks it possible and important to say something about Jesus' developing God-consciousness. He does not, however, turn his back on classical Christology. Though he argues that there are significant weaknesses in Chalcedon's Christology, he also acknowledges its continuing significance. In place of Chalcedon's formula of "two natures in one person," Sobrino prefers to speak of Jesus' personal oneness with the Father, a oneness that Jesus expressed in the radical way in which he lived for other people and identified with the poor and oppressed.

Perhaps the best-known African American liberation theologian is James Cone, whose *God of the Oppressed* carefully develops the argument that Jesus is "black":

> My point is that God came, and continues to come, to those who are poor and helpless, for the purpose of setting them free. And since the people of color are his elected poor in America, any interpretation of God that ignores black oppression cannot be Christian theology. The "blackness of Christ," therefore, is not simply a statement about skin color, but rather the transcendent affirmation that God has not ever, no not ever, left the oppressed alone in struggle.[7]

Like Sobrino, Cone has little interest in theological speculation about the relation between Jesus' two natures. The figure of Jesus is important for Christian faith because he is always the black Christ who provides oppressed people the soul necessary for acts of resistance and liberation. For Cone, Jesus Christ is "black" in that he identifies with those who are oppressed by ideologies that rob people of their basic humanity, such as racism and sexism. The "blackness" of Jesus is not a statement about Jesus' skin color, but a description of his social status as one who was rejected by the religious establishment and executed by the ruling political authorities.

Liberation Christology has already made important contributions by reminding the church that questions about the true identity of Jesus of Nazareth are also radical questions about the nature of discipleship and the mission of the church. Liberation Christology continually reminds all churches, especially white affluent churches, of the demanding, difficult gospel that Jesus preached and lived. If that gospel were proclaimed today in all its offensiveness, there might well be many people with great possessions, like the man who asked Jesus what he had to do to inherit eternal life (Mark 10:17–22), who would turn away from Christian faith in sorrow. Liberation Christology will not allow churches to accommodate the demands of the gospel to societies and economies that have turned their backs on the poor and hid their eyes from the oppressed.

Although liberation Christology has made important contributions to the church's understanding of Jesus and to issues of Christian ethics, it has not yet offered a clear description of Jesus' relation to the one he calls Father. Sobrino's books have been a significant step in that direction, but neither he nor Cone nor other liberation theologians have interpreted the biblical claim that Jesus is "God with us" in a manner that is consistent with the faith of the ancient church. The Jesus of liberation theology often seems to be more like one of Israel's prophets than the Word made flesh.

What Do Theologians Do with an Apocalyptic Jesus?

A fourth type of contemporary Christology emphasizes the importance of eschatology.

For much of the New Testament, as we have seen, Jesus' resurrection means that his story does not end with his death. The

Jesus who preached and enacted the kingdom of God is revealed to be the one who has brought and will yet bring that kingdom. The Jesus who, in the language of the Apostles' Creed, has "ascended into heaven, and sitteth on the right hand of God the Father Almighty," is also the one who "shall come to judge the quick and the dead." Christian hope is not hope in what has been, but hope in the Jesus who is coming again, and who in his final coming, according to the apostle Paul, will hand over the kingdom to God the Father "after he has destroyed every ruler and every authority and power," and then and only then will God be "all in all" (1 Corinthians 15:24, 28).

But after two thousand years of human history, what are Christians to do with this apocalyptic Jesus? In the last third of the twentieth century, several theologians have made eschatology a central theme in their interpretations of Jesus as the Christ. Like many forms of liberation Christology, they begin "below," with the historical Jesus, and discover his uniqueness and significance as Lord in his "openness" to God and his complete dedication to the coming kingdom of God. This interpretation of Jesus as Christ does not begin "from above," with the incarnation, but with Jesus of Nazareth in his historical particularity. It also pays close attention to the central role that the kingdom of God plays in Jesus' ministry, and it does not evade either the early church's apocalyptic expectation that the kingdom is near or the equally important need to reinterpret that claim in terms that are intelligible to modern people. Language about Jesus' "openness" to God and God's promised future has provided the different forms of this type of Christology with an idiom for reinterpreting first-century Christian language, especially the biblical language of hope.

Wolfhart Pannenberg and Jürgen Moltmann are two German theologians who represent different forms of eschatological Christology. Pannenberg interprets Jesus' resurrection as a "proleptic" event, an event in human history that points toward and anticipates in the present the coming kingdom of God. Moltmann's eschatology is more "messianic," more directly related to Jewish apocalyptic, and emphasizes hope in a kingdom of God that is not a remote reality in some distant future, not some utopia toward which history is slowly moving or the meaning of universal history, but hope in a Messiah and his kingdom that are coming to the present and fill it with an expectation and urgency, an urgency that has ethical and social implications.

In *Jesus—God and Man* (German, 1964) and more recently in the second volume of his three-volume *Systematic Theology* (1991), Pannenberg insists that it is Jesus' resurrection from the dead that discloses his true identity as Christ and Son of God. Jesus does not become the Christ in the resurrection, except in the subjective understanding of those who believe in him.[8] That might seem to suggest that the resurrected Jesus was "adopted" by God as the Christ, but the resurrection reveals who Jesus truly is and always has been throughout his life, ministry, and death. As Pannenberg puts it in his *Systematic Theology*, "The Easter event became the starting point of apostolic proclamation and the church's Christology. Both rest on the distinctive significance of this event in its reference back to the pre-Easter history of Jesus."[9] The resurrection, therefore, is the basis for the New Testament's response to questions about Jesus' identity, questions that the early church answers by means of the incarnation and the nativity stories in Matthew and Luke. From the beginning this Jesus was "God with us" (Matthew 1:23).

In his *Systematic Theology*, Pannenberg divides his Christology into three parts. First, like many other contemporary theologians, Pannenberg begins with Jesus' humanity, with anthropology—not with anthropology in general, but with anthropology "from below," with the particular human history of Jesus, with "the man Jesus and his story."[10] In the whole course of his life, Jesus is the "new man," the second Adam. He is "the original of a new humanity that is made anew in his image by participation in his obedience, in his death and resurrection."[11] His identity cannot be known apart from his history, and especially "its outcome in the passion and the Easter event." It is only in light of the historical event of his resurrection—an event that Pannenberg believes to be open to historical inquiry and argument—that we may say "that the child Jesus who was born of Mary was the Messiah and the Son of God."[12] Second, only after discussing Jesus' humanity does Pannenberg turn to his deity, not as something added to his humanity, but in order to find his eternal sonship in the reality of his human life. Jesus' deity is his unity with God. As in the case of his humanity, so too with his deity it is his resurrection that reveals the meaning of his ministry and who he is in relation to God. The incarnation is God's "self-actualization" in the world. Finally, Jesus brings universal salvation in the form of reconciliation with God. Fellowship with Christ mediates fellowship with God and "a renewal of fellowship with others."[13]

Eschatology is also a major theme in Jürgen Moltmann's theology and is central to his Christology. In 1964 Moltmann published *Theology of Hope*, which rooted Christian hope in Jesus' resurrection, understood eschatologically.[14] In 1996, thirty-two years later, Moltmann returned to the same themes in *The Coming of God*. In a sense the two books stand as bookends to Moltmann's theological career. The second title is significant. The God we know in Jesus Christ, the God who raised him from the dead, is both triune and a "coming" God, not a God who exists in some distant, remote future but a God who is coming and who has promised to transform all things. Both these themes, resurrection and eschatology, are important for understanding Moltmann's Christology.

Moltmann's second major book, *The Crucified God* (1972), argues that Jesus' death on the cross means that pain, suffering, and death are not something alien to God but are events in the very life, history, and being of the Trinity.[15] Much like Martin Luther, Moltmann's interpretation of Christian faith is above all else a theology of the cross. Christian reflection about God and the world must begin and end at the foot of the cross. Insofar as Jesus is Emmanuel, "God with us" (Matthew 1:23), then Jesus' death means that he suffers abandonment by the Father, and that the Father suffers the loss of the Son. Jesus' cry of dereliction in Mark 15:34 is a significant text for Moltmann. Jesus' suffering and death are not simply something he experienced in his human nature. In Chalcedon's language, Jesus is one person, and that means his two natures cannot be separated from one another, but each communes or shares with the other. Consequently his divine nature shares in what he experiences in his humanity. His despair, reflected in his cry of abandonment, is not something that he experiences only in his humanity; his deity participates in that suffering as well. This leads Moltmann to argue that the classical Christian claim that God is "immutable" and without passions is incompatible with the God described in the Bible, the God of the Hebrew prophets, who is a God of great pathos and who weeps over Israel, the God of Jesus Christ, who is a God of suffering love. A God who cannot suffer, Moltmann insists, is a God who cannot love. If "God," in light of Jesus' resurrection, is understood as a Trinity of three persons in a community of mutual, reciprocal (perichoretic) love, then the event of the cross means that the Father suffers passionately the loss of the Son. Death becomes an event in the divine life of God that is overcome only by the Spirit of life.

Moltmann's *The Way of Jesus Christ: Christology in Messianic Dimensions* (1989) is his first full treatment of Christology.[16] The words "way" and "messianic" in the title and subtitle are important in his interpretation of Jesus. He begins by discussing "the messianic perspective." He rejects the categories of "from above" and "from below" and proposes a Christology "*in the eschatological history of God*"—a Christology that is cosmic in its scope, encompassing the history of both human beings and nature. In this "history," Jesus is "on the road" or on his "way" with the Father and the Spirit. Hence Moltmann proposes a thoroughly Trinitarian Christology, one that begins with the Spirit (because Jesus' history in the Gospels begins with the Spirit) and as such is a pneumatological Christology.[17] It is a history or "story," Moltmann argues, and as such it must be told sequentially. It is the eschatological history of God: it begins with Jesus' messianic mission to the poor, then moves to Jesus' apocalyptic passion on the cross, and culminates in the transfiguring resurrection of Jesus from the dead. Jesus' cross and resurrection are mutually related: the one must be understood in relation to the other. However, "God's raising of Jesus was the foundation for faith in Christ" and also the foundation of the church. "Christian faith," therefore, "stands or falls with Christ's resurrection." Christ's resurrection is an "apocalyptic happening," and as such it is a qualitatively different event than Jesus' death. Jesus' death is the end of history while the resurrection, understood apocalyptically, is "the beginning of the new creation of the world."[18]

The resurrection has cosmic consequences not only for human beings but for nature as well. In a comment (perhaps directed at Pannenberg) Moltmann writes, "Anyone who describes Christ's resurrection as 'historical,' in just the same way as his death on the cross, is overlooking the new creation which the resurrection begins, and is falling short of the eschatological hope."[19]

Is a Male Christ Relevant to Women?

Yet another type of contemporary Christology that developed in the last third of the twentieth century is feminist Christology. The context for feminist theology is the pervasive reality of patriarchy, understood simply as the assumption that the male gender is to be valued and privileged more highly than the female. Patriarchal societies are structured so that it is more likely that men rather than women will exercise political, social, and economic power. Patriarchy, therefore, is deeply embedded in human history and in most forms of human consciousness. The social protests in Western Europe and North America in the 1960s, precipitated by the American War in Vietnam and African American struggles for civil rights in the United States, called all established social and political institutions into question, including the churches, and challenged long-held assumptions about race, class, and gender. It was in that period of social ferment and consciousness-raising that a new wave of feminism emerged, and with it the first attempts at feminist theology, initially in figures such as Mary Daly, Rosemary Radford Ruether, and Elisabeth Schüssler Fiorenza. In *Beyond God the Father*, Daly coined the phrase that summed up the concerns of many feminist theologians: "If God is male, then the male is God."[20] In other words, sexism is a debilitating form of idolatry, and both males and females must be freed from its captivity.

The pervasiveness of patriarchy posed a significant challenge for feminist theologians. Each had to decide whether patriarchy is so deeply entrenched that Christian faith could not be extricated from it and thus was beyond reform. Some, like Mary Daly, did conclude that Christianity could not be "saved" and began doing theology outside of the Christian tradition in communities that sought to recover a female spirituality that celebrated goddess figures. Other feminist theologians remained Christian and have tried to reconstruct Christian faith and theology "root and branch." Reconstructing Christian theology has been a formidable challenge for feminists, and a central issue in that task has been the figure of Jesus Christ. Because he is so central to Christian faith, as we recognized in chapter 1, and because Jesus of Nazareth is male, Christology more than perhaps any other doctrine posed the greatest challenge to feminist Christian theologians. Rosemary Radford Ruether put the question succinctly in *Sexism and God-Talk*, "Can a Male Savior Save Women?"[21]

For Ruether, like many other feminist theologians, because the Bible and Christian theology were written in patriarchal cultures, they may be sources for reconstructing theology in general and Christology in particular, but they cannot be normative. To make them normative would be to reaffirm patriarchy. Consequently a new norm must be found. Like the first and second types of Christology (see above), Ruether makes experience the norm for feminist theology, but not just any form of experience: "The uniqueness of feminist theology lies not in its use of the criterion of experience but rather in its use of *women's* experience, which has been almost entirely shut out of theological reflection in the past."[22] She proposes that the norm or "critical principle" for feminist theology is "the promotion of the full humanity of women." Consequently, "whatever denies, diminishes, or distorts the full humanity of women is, therefore, appraised as not redemptive." Or put positively, "what does promote the full humanity of women is of the Holy."[23] This formal principle begs the question of what constitutes "the full humanity of women." Ruether finds this norm in the prophetic-liberating traditions of the Bible. Insofar as biblical texts reflect this normative principle, "they are regarded as authoritative." If they do not so reflect, they "are to be frankly set aside and rejected."[24] Prophetic-liberating traditions recognize God's vindication of the oppressed, criticize dominant systems of power, envision a new age of God's peace and justice, and denounce ideologies that justify unjust systems.[25]

After tracing the development of the patriarchalization of Christology, Ruether considers two alternatives in the Christian tradition. Androgynous Christologies, found especially in Gnosticism and some forms of Christian mysticism, include both genders but still have an androcentric bias because Christ is associated with maleness. Consequently women, even though they are included in an androgynous Christ, still cannot represent full human potential. In Spirit Christologies, on the other hand, Christ is found in a new humanity that "discloses the future potential of redeemed life."[26] Christ is discovered in early Christian charismatic movements such as Montanism, where the risen Christ continues to speak directly to Christians. The problem with Spirit Christology is that it separates the past revelation of Christ in the historical Jesus from new movements of the Spirit, movements such as feminism, and leads to a revolt against the Jesus of the Gospels. Over against both of these alternatives, Ruether suggests a new way of doing feminist Christology, one that appeals to the Jesus of the Synoptic Gospels, a prophetic Jesus who does not justify the status quo but "speaks on behalf of the marginalized and despised groups of society." And one of the groups most obviously marginalized in the first century is women.

Hence Ruether—along with Sobrino, Cone, and Moltmann—embraces the image of Jesus as Liberator. Ruether's Jesus renounces the patriarchal system of domination and embodies in his own person "the new humanity of service and mutual empowerment," which seems to be Ruether's understanding of the kingdom of God. The maleness of Jesus "has no ultimate significance." Both Jesus, "the homeless Jewish prophet, and the marginalized women and men who respond to him represent the overthrow of the present world system and the sign of a dawning new age in which God's will is done on earth." The Word of God, therefore, is not "encapsulated" in the historical Jesus. The Christian community, liberated from patriarchy and for inclusivity, "continues Christ's identity."[27] This community is not the church of institutionalized patriarchy, but those prophetic communities committed to justice and inclusivity.

In *She Who Is*, Elizabeth A. Johnson, like Ruether, reconstructs Christology on the basis of the criterion of "the emancipation of women toward human flourishing." That implies neither reverse sexism (matriarchy replacing patriarchy) nor a sameness that denies gender distinctions. The goal is "not to make women equal partners in an oppressive system," but to transform the system into a nonhierarchical one that promotes "the full flourishing of all beings in their uniqueness and interrelation."[28] In order to accomplish that goal, Johnson invokes the wisdom tradition, a pervasive theme in Scripture, and argues that "Jesus is Sophia incarnate, the Wisdom of God."[29] Jesus, therefore, is "the prophet and child of Sophia sent to announce that God is the God of all-inclusive love who wills the wholeness and humanity of everyone, especially the poor and heavy-burdened."

For Johnson only a "naïve physicalism" would "collapse the totality of the Christ into the human man Jesus." Biblical metaphors, such as the Paul's body of Christ and John's vine and branches, "expand the reality of Christ to include potentially all of redeemed humanity, sisters and brothers, still on the way." Consequently "the biblical symbol Christ, the one anointed in the Spirit, cannot be restricted to the historical person Jesus nor to certain select members of the community but signifies all those who by drinking of the Spirit participate in the community of disciples." In Johnson's wisdom Christology, "Jesus is named the Christ in a paradigmatic way," but texts such as Matthew 25:31–46 suggest that "the focus is not on Jesus alone in a sort of Jesus-ology, but on looking with him in the same direction toward the inclusive well-being of the body of Christ." The story of Jesus-Sophia cannot be limited to Jesus but "goes on in history as the story of the whole Christ, *christa* and *christus* alike, the wisdom community."[30]

Christian feminist theologians rightly recognize that if Christian faith is to be freed from patriarchy, Christology is a crucial issue. It must be reconstructed in such a manner that maleness is not paradigmatic of the divine. Daly was right. "If God is male, then the male is God." And if the man Jesus is, in Matthew's words, Emmanuel, or "God with us," then the dots do seem to connect maleness with divinity. Feminist Christology cannot deny that Jesus of Nazareth was male, but it must argue that Jesus' maleness is irrelevant to his identity as the Christ. One way, but by no means the only way, to do that is to argue that the figure of Sophia, or Wisdom, identifies Jesus rather than having Jesus identify Wisdom. That appears to be one of the moves Johnson makes in describing Jesus as "Jesus-Sophia." The problem, however, is that Paul did not argue that the wisdom of God discloses the identity of Jesus. To the contrary, he argues that the foolishness of Jesus' cross reveals the wisdom of God. In Johnson's version of Wisdom Christology, Jesus seems to be captive to a particular social agenda: the construction of a human community characterized by mutuality, reciprocity, and inclusiveness. Jesus, then, is the paradigmatic example of the Spirit insofar as he represents and advocates those values. He is not, however, allowed to call them into question or specify what might be involved in realizing them. If he does so, he can no longer be the paradigmatic instance of Wisdom. James Cone once wrote that "if Jesus is white and not black, he is an oppressor, and we must kill him."[31] For both Cone and Johnson, Jesus is "paradigmatic" only insofar as he supports the values and goals to which they are so passionately committed.

What Is Narrative Christology?

In addition to these five types of contemporary Christology, a sixth has emerged in the last third of the twentieth century. It focuses on biblical narratives, especially the narratives of the Gospels. It assumes that the identity of Jesus as the Christ is disclosed in these narratives and that these same narratives have the capacity to transform the identities of persons and communities.

Two important theological sources for the emergence of narrative Christology are the Swiss theologian Karl Barth and the American theologian H. Richard Niebuhr. The most important Protestant theologian since Calvin, Barth recast Chalcedonian Christology in volume 4 of his *Church Dogmatics* by interpreting

Christ's two natures dialectically.[32] In volume 4/1 he describes Jesus' deity (his lordship) in relation to his humanity (his servanthood). Jesus is the Lord as servant. In volume 4/2 he interprets Jesus' humanity in relation to his deity, and Jesus is the servant as Lord. Furthermore, in each case Barth uses the Gospel narratives to interpret what "Lord" and "servant" mean and how they are related to one another. More than any other theologian in the modern period, Barth uses the Bible, especially Gospel narratives, not to illustrate his interpretation of Jesus, but as the basis for his constructive Christology.

In *The Meaning of Revelation*, Niebuhr argues that revelation occurs when the events of what he calls "external history" cease to be only objective facts and become subjectively significant for personal and communal identity.[33] When that happens, when historical events become part of a person's and a community's identity, when they become events in what Niebuhr describes as "the story of the heart"—then they become the lenses through which self-understanding and identity are understood. Niebuhr's "story of the heart" was deeply informed by Augustine's *Confessions* and by Calvin's understanding of the Christian life as a journey or pilgrimage in which individuals and communities become conformed to Jesus Christ.

Both Barth and Niebuhr emphasize the importance of narrative for interpreting Christian faith, but as we have seen in chapter 2, there is not just one narrative or story in the Bible but several. In the New Testament, Gospel narratives are indispensable for understanding Jesus' identity, but there are various forms of narrative in the Gospels and in the larger canon as well. For example, some stories that Jesus tells take the form of a parable. More often than not, when Jesus proclaims the kingdom of God, he does so by means of parables, but what do they suggest about who Jesus is? One possibility, proposed by several theologians, is that Jesus is not only a teller of parables, but he is himself *the* parable of God. Some New Testament scholars have proposed that parables are not so much allegories, in which the story is simply an illustration of a larger point or lesson that transcends the story, as they are "extended metaphors." The parables are metaphors in that they are stories about familiar situations and settings—the ordinary world of first-century Israel—but in these stories something wholly unexpected, something truly extraordinary, erupts in this ordinary world and transforms it. A shepherd loses a sheep, a traveler is robbed and beaten, a young man demands his inheritance and squanders it, and the owner of a vineyard hires laborers to harvest his grapes. Each of these would have been an everyday situation to Jesus' audience. In each parable, however, there is a surprise, a shocking development: The shepherd will go to any length to rescue the lost sheep. The traveler who has been beaten and robbed is rescued by a despised foreigner. The father runs to welcome home his wayward son. The owner of the vineyard pays his laborers the same wage regardless of how long they have worked. Each of these parables is a story that Jesus tells about the kingdom of God, a kingdom that is near at hand.

But what if Jesus is not simply a teller of parables about God's kingdom, but is himself the parable of God's kingdom (see chapter 2)? At first glance there is nothing exceptional about Jesus. The Gospels tell us that the reaction from his neighbors in Nazareth to his proclamation of God's kingdom is dismay and disbelief. "Is not this the carpenter's son?" (Matthew 13:55). And yet in the life, death, and resurrection of this ordinary, everyday first-century Galilean Jew, something extraordinary becomes apparent: this thoroughly human Jesus, the carpenter's son, is at the same time "God with us" (Matthew 1:23). To understand Jesus as God's parable, as God's extended metaphor, is to interpret him quite differently than Chalcedon did.

Other theologians find it significant that Jesus' parables occur amid the larger narratives of the Gospels themselves and that it is only in these more-encompassing stories that we can properly understand the parables. Although the Gospels are written for different communities, which are facing different kinds of problems, at the center of them stands the figure of Jesus of Nazareth, who is both familiar and strange, one who proclaims both the unbounded reach of God's love and the nearness of God's judgment. Jesus has a different look about him in each of the Gospels, as we observed in chapter 2, but in their own way Mark, Matthew, Luke, and John tell their respective stories about Jesus for two common purposes: to tell readers why the church believes Jesus to be the Christ, the redeeming presence of God, and to tell them what follows from the confession that Jesus is Lord—the call to discipleship.

Obviously not everything in the New Testament is a story. Does the focus on the narratives of the Gospels mean that those nonnarrative texts—Paul's Letters, for example—are unimportant? Not at all. Paul provides the theological categories—for example, the second Adam, the righteousness of faith, the significance of the law, the freedom of Christ—for the proper interpretation of the Gospels' narratives. It may be self-evident to some contemporary Christians that Jesus' cross means that humanity's relationship to God is no longer determined by the extent to which anyone obeys God's law, but in first-century Israel that was not at all self-evident. Paul presupposes the stories of the Gospels and interprets them to mean that sinners are made righteous before God solely by Jesus Christ's faith and obedience. Paul's Letters, therefore, are indispensable for understanding the meaning of the Gospels' stories about Jesus.

Narrative Christology is similar to some of the types of contemporary Christology we have already examined, but it also differs from them in several important respects. It resembles them in that most forms of narrative theology do not use metaphysical categories or the language of the classical creeds in interpreting Jesus' identity. Although Scripture does not directly answer many of the questions that evoked the church's creeds and confessions, it does share a general concern with them: the question of Jesus' true identity. And most importantly, Scripture answers that question differently than do most forms of classical Christology. The New Testament Gospels do not identify Jesus by means of theological propositions and philosophical categories. Rather, they do so by means of stories—both large and small—that report and interpret the decisive events in Jesus' personal history. While the classical creeds make theological assertions, the Gospels tell stories, and the two modes of discourse are quite different.

Narrative Christology is not simply a form of storytelling, not simply a matter of repeating Gospel stories about Jesus. It works with Scripture differently than do other forms of Christology, both classical and contemporary. Almost every theological interpretation of Jesus claims to be guided and informed by the witness of Scripture. Narrative Christology, however, takes biblical narratives as its primary evidence and answers questions about Jesus' identity by working directly with those texts.

An important difference between narrative Christology and other forms of contemporary Christology is that it does not try to get "behind" the stories of the Bible to the real Jesus—that is, the "historical" Jesus. It begins with the conviction that the basis for Christology is not some elusive historical figure that stands *behind* Scripture but the figure that is identified *in* Scripture. On the one hand, this recognizes Scripture for what it is: a confession of faith and not a biography (see chapter 1). At the same time it must be acknowledged that some forms of narrative Christology muddy the water on this point and do not clarify the difference between the Jesus of history and the Jesus of the Gospel narratives. Both Karl Barth and Hans Frei, for example, argue that biblical narratives are neither history nor myth, but a curious form of narrative that Frei describes as "history-like."[34] The theological problem that such a claim creates is that it appears to call into question the basic Christian belief that God's redemptive activity has taken place in particular historical events. If the basis for identifying Jesus and the meaning of salvation is a narrative that is not history but only history-like, it follows that the redemptive events are also not history but only history-like. Such a claim could be interpreted as a form of Docetism and would be vulnerable to many of the criticisms we discussed in chapter 4. Not all forms of narrative Christology argue that biblical narrative is history-like. It is possible to agree that primary attention should be given to what biblical narrative says about Jesus Christ, but at the same time to acknowledge that this Jesus is also a historical figure and that historical inquiry plays an important but limited role in helping the reader know who the Jesus of the text is. A narrative Christology of this sort would employ the methods of both literary and historical analysis of Scripture.

How does narrative Christology identify Jesus as the Christ? One answer to that question is given by Hans Frei's book *The Identity of Jesus Christ*. Frei believes that the Gospels give the reader a story that identifies Jesus by means of several interrelated stages.[35] The first consists of the birth and infancy stories about Jesus. Here Jesus does not really have his own identity. As we noted in chapter 2, in the nativity stories Jesus receives his identity from the history of Israel. The history, traditions, and faith of Israel give Jesus his identity. He is not an individual in his own right but the history of Israel writ small in the person of a single Jewish child. Jesus is the fulfillment of the prophecies of Israel, but it is primarily those prophecies that give Jesus his identity as the Messiah or Christ.

The second stage of the Gospel narratives extends from Jesus' baptism by John the Baptist to his decision to carry his ministry from Galilee to Jerusalem. In this stage of the story, Jesus begins to appear as his own person. He is the one who appears in Galilee, preaching the nearness of the kingdom of God, and his strange and marvelous acts are signs of the inbreaking of God's rule. Here Jesus is much more of an individual than he was in the infancy stories, but still not yet fully himself. He is the one who comes and proclaims God's kingdom, but it is the kingdom that identifies Jesus rather than Jesus identifying the kingdom.

The third and final stage of the story is Jesus' passion and resurrection. Here the wheel comes full circle. In the events of his trial, crucifixion, and especially his resurrection, Jesus is most fully himself. Frei argues that it is here that the true meanings of christological titles such as "Messiah/Christ," "Son of God," and "Lord" are disclosed. It is no longer the titles that give Jesus his identity. Now it is Jesus, crucified and raised, who discloses the true meanings of the titles. Jesus is not just the long-awaited Messiah but the crucified Messiah, and as the apostle Paul understood, a stumbling block to Jews and folly to Gentiles. Similarly, it is no longer the coming kingdom of God that gives Jesus his identity, as in the second part of the story. Now it is the crucified and risen Jesus who identifies the kingdom. From the perspective of the whole of the Gospel narrative, the Jesus who came proclaiming the kingdom of God is himself revealed to be the kingdom. And finally it is no longer Israel who gives Jesus his identity, as in the first stage of the story, but now, from the perspective of the narrative in its entirety, all the promises of God to Israel come to fruition in this Jesus, and it is this Jesus who is now seen to be the destiny and identity of Israel.

Although Jesus' identity is fully disclosed only in the final stage of the story, it must not be separated from the first two stages. Jesus is most fully himself in his death and resurrection, but the final stage of the story is unintelligible apart from the rest of the narrative. Thus an important reversal takes place in Jesus' passion and resurrection. In his death and resurrection, he finally assumes his own unique and unsubstitutable identity, but who he truly is cannot be understood apart from the infancy stories and the history of Israel and his ministry as the one who proclaims and enacts the kingdom of God. Without the latter the reversal would not be possible, and Jesus' identity as the crucified One would have nothing to do with either the history of Israel or the kingdom of God. We have already discussed some of the dire consequences of separating the cross and resurrection from Jesus' teaching and healing ministry. If the final stage of the story is separated from Jesus' embodiment of the kingdom of God, then the church runs the high risk of forgetting that Christology and discipleship are inseparable.

Finally, narrative Christology offers some tantalizing possibilities for reinterpreting the incarnation. In the early twenty-first century, how should we understand Paul's claim that "in Christ God was reconciling the world to himself" (2 Corinthians 5:19)? From the perspective of narrative Christology, this central Christian confession does not mean that there was some part of Jesus of Nazareth that was divine. The incarnation means quite simply that the identity of Jesus, as narrated in the Gospels, is also the disclosure of the identity of God. The Gospels not only identify Jesus; they also identify him as the enacted intention of God and as such the very reality of God. Karl Barth described God as "being in act," and Jesus of Nazareth is what God intends—

God's love and freedom—enacted and embodied in history. Personal identity takes the form of a narrative, and the incarnation is the Christian confession that the biblical narratives identifying Jesus also disclose the identity of God. Jesus is most fully himself in the resurrection because in that single event God's deepest intentions are identified with Jesus of Nazareth. The resurrection directs the reader's attention back to the Gospel story as a whole, and it underlies the Christian confession that in Jesus' narrative identity, the world encounters the reality of God.

Like other contemporary attempts to interpret Jesus' identity, narrative Christology suggests new possibilities for reinterpreting the church's classical confessions, but it also has problems that remain unresolved. Not the least of these is the elusiveness of the term "narrative." Often when theologians use the term "narrative," it is unclear what they mean. In the case of narrative Christology, for example, the term "biblical narrative" sometimes refers to specific biblical texts, and at other times it appears to refer to a "narrative" that cannot be identified with a particular Gospel or a specific biblical text but is somehow a synthesis or "harmony" of all of them. The "biblical narrative" that gives Jesus his identity becomes not Mark or John or any other particular Gospel, but a narrative that is actually not a text except in the imagination of the theologian. The important differences in how the Gospels identify Jesus are used at best selectively, or they disappear altogether in the harmonized narrative. This ambiguity in "biblical narrative" is related to the ambiguity in the historical character of the narrative.

These are only a few of the difficult problems that narrative Christology must untangle. At the same time, narrative Christology provides an interesting possibility for the reinterpretation of the church's classical creeds and its claims about the meaning of incarnation, atonement, and salvation. Protestant theology has often discovered that when it encounters an apparent impasse, the resolution of that dilemma is found in a fresh return to Scripture and its witness to Jesus as the Christ.

Chapter Six

Who Is Jesus Christ in a Pluralistic World?

What Challenges Does Today's World Pose for Christian Faith?

We return to the question with which we began in chapter 1: "Who is Jesus Christ for us today?" For two reasons many Christians today think differently about this question than did previous generations. First, "today's world" in this question has changed. It is a different world from earlier days. Both our perception of it and the world itself have changed. It may be true that Jesus Christ is the same yesterday, today, and tomorrow, but because the world in which Christians live today has moved beneath their feet, they must speak of Jesus differently than they once did if they want this new world to hear and understand the good news about him. As the Word made flesh, Jesus always speaks directly to specific people living in particular situations. If they are to be faithful to the tasks to which God calls them, Christians must ask who Christ is for today's new world.

The second reason Christians think about this question differently has to do with the term "us." Before the last half of the twentieth century, when many Western Christians heard this question, they assumed that "us" referred to people in the Western world. They knew there was more to the world than Western Europe and North America, but those who were not white,

Western, and Christian were considered "foreign." They lived in another world. Protestant denominations had Boards of Foreign Missions to deal with that other world, and the term "us" referred to "civilized" Christians, Christians in the Western world, who had been commissioned by Christ to go and teach that other, "foreign" world about Jesus and "to make disciples of all nations" (Matthew 28:19–20). Before the last half of the twentieth century, it did not occur to many Christians that the day was soon coming when there would be more Christians in the non-Western world than in the West, and that the church there would grow faster and exhibit greater vitality than the older, long-established churches of the West.

When contemporary Christians ask, "Who is Jesus Christ for us today?" many recognize they can no longer assume that they know to whom the "us" refers. The question is now heard and answered differently by different groups of Christians. If the "us" refers to Christians in Kenya or in Korea, the question is going to be understood differently than it will be by Anglicans worshiping in nearly empty churches in London. If the "us" refers to immigrant, nonwhite churches in urban America, it will be understood differently than it will be by Presbyterians in small towns in rural Georgia.

The world is different today because large demographic, social, and cultural changes have occurred. By the end of the twentieth century, many countries in Western Europe and North America were rapidly becoming more diverse racially and ethnically than they had been at the beginning of the century. The United States, for example, is now dramatically more diverse ethnically, racially, and religiously than it was a hundred years ago. Throughout its history it has experienced waves of immigration. In the nineteenth century those waves consisted largely of ethnic groups from Western and Eastern Europe. In the last half of the twentieth century, growing numbers of Asians, Hispanics, and other groups also began to enter the United States. The White Anglo-Saxon Protestant (WASP) community began to shrink in comparison to rapidly increasing numbers from other ethnic groups. Hispanics, for example, are currently the fastest growing ethnic group in the United States. By the middle of the twenty-first century, Caucasians may be a minority in the United States. Many American cities that had no Buddhist temples or Muslim mosques at the beginning of the twentieth century now have several.

Not only have North America and Western Europe become more diverse; at the same time the world also has changed. It has become both larger and smaller. At the beginning of the twentieth century, travel to distant countries took several days or weeks. By the end of the century, those same destinations could be reached in not weeks but a few hours. At the beginning of the century, travel to the moon was considered science fiction. By the last third of the century, it was a reality. With the explosion of the Internet and other forms of information technology in the last decades of the twentieth century, there is now almost-instant communication anywhere on the globe. Furthermore, information about almost anything is now accessible to more people than ever before. In order to learn something about food production in China, it is no longer necessary to go to the nearest library. That information is now available on the Internet at the click of a mouse. The world has become smaller: it is more accessible to us now than it ever has been.

The world has also become larger and more complex. We know more about ourselves and our world than we ever have. Far more people today know that there is a difference between Sunni and Shiite Muslims than they did before 1991. The Internet now enables anyone to see streets and neighborhoods anywhere in the world. Both the local communities in which we live and our larger world have become significantly more complex than they were a hundred years ago. Many local communities are significantly less homogeneous today than they once were, in part because new groups have moved in, in part because we now know that there was always more diversity in the community than many realized. A hundred years ago many people assumed that nearly everyone in the United States was either Caucasian or African American, Christian, and heterosexual. That is no longer true. Most people now understand that their communities are diverse in many ways, including race, ethnicity, and sexual orientation.

What Do These Global Changes Mean for Christology?

In this new world two issues now dominate discussions of Christology. The first concerns the interpretation of Jesus by Christians who have not previously participated in academic discussions of Christology. Many are from outside Western Europe and North America. They may live in churches that were started by Western missionaries during the nineteenth and early twentieth centuries; by the late twentieth century, if not before, these churches began to develop their own theological identities and interpretations of the gospel by using their own cultural symbols and not those of Western Christianity. In addition, some Christians in Western Europe and North America who had not previously participated in conversations about Christology began to add their voices to the discussion: for example, immigrants from all over the world in Western Europe and African Americans, Hispanics, Native Americans, and gays and lesbians in North America.

The second issue has to do with the Christian claim that Jesus is the Savior of the world and what that claim implies for Christian relations with other religious traditions and communities. For many Christians, the issue is sometimes described as the "finality" of Jesus Christ. Is Jesus of Nazareth the "final"—as in ultimate or normative—revelation of God? Is faith in him the only means of salvation? In John's Gospel, Christians read that Jesus said: "I am the light of the world. Whoever follows me will never walk in darkness but will have the light of life" (8:12). "I am the way, and the truth, and the life. No one comes to the Father except through me" (14:6). If Jesus is the one Word of God (1:1–5, 14) and the one "Savior of the world" (4:42), are other religions inferior forms of faith? Does that then mean that Christians have nothing to learn about God from them and should seek only to convert them to Christian faith?

Because the globe has become both smaller and larger, both of these concerns—the development of Christology in new churches and the relation of Christology to other religious communities—have sometimes been described as the "contextualization" or indigenization" or "enculturation" of Christian faith.

The contextualization of Christian faith is not something that "outsiders" can do. It can only be done by those Christians who live in a particular communal and cultural setting: hence the importance of the "us." The question "Who is Jesus Christ for us today?" when asked by Christians in East Africa or Korea, cannot be answered by Christians in Western Europe or North America because they are not the "us." The question can only be answered by those who live in these communities and who participate in those experiences and histories.

The contextualization of Christian faith is not simply a sociological issue, although the tools of cultural anthropology can help a community (including those in Western Europe and North America) understand some of the difficult issues it faces in appropriating Jesus Christ for contemporary life. In its most important sense, contextualization is theological. As we have seen, Christians believe that the incarnation affirms that the Word became flesh in Jesus of Nazareth—in a particular man at a particular moment in history. Incarnation is not a general statement. The Word is not revealed in humanity as such, but in a particular person, and that particularity is also the scandal and offense of Christian faith. Christians also believe that Jesus of Nazareth is a resurrected and living Christ and that by means of his Spirit he continues to address people today. Contextualization, therefore, affirms that the Word of God is no less incarnational today than it was in the first century. God's Word, revealed in Jesus of Nazareth, continues to address human beings in a rich diversity of historical, racial, and ethnic contexts, and the challenge to every Christian community is how to understand the Word addressed to it in ways that are intelligible to its larger culture. Although much can be learned from other churches that have faced this challenge in the past, each church today must do so in ways that are appropriate to its particular history and culture, using symbols and concepts that people in their setting can understand. Just as many Presbyterians in the United States at the beginning of the twenty-first century have difficulty understanding the Westminster Confession of Faith of the seventeenth century, so too Christians in East Africa and

Korea have difficulty understanding Christian faith as it has been developed in Western Europe and the United States.

In 1989 Stearn Publishers Limited published a book titled *The Faces of Jesus*, with over 150 images of Jesus—paintings, watercolors, sculptures in wood, metal, stone and ivory, frescos, silk, stained glass, and so forth—from early Christianity and the medieval period to the present, and from Western Europe, North America, and Russia, but also from China, Japan, Africa, the Philippines, Mexico, and so forth. The photography was by Lee Boltin, and the commentary on the images was written by Frederick Buechner. One image is a wood carving of the face of a black Jesus by an anonymous African artist. Buechner writes:

> You ache to run your fingers down the bridge of the nose and the great, full lips; to trace the cool plane of the cheeks where the swirl of the grain has become the track of dried tears, the scar running down into one eyebrow where the wood has cracked. There is no way of saying all that shines out of such a face other than the way the wood has said it. . . . The wood is mute. What it tells us is simply all there is to tell about what it means to be black, what it means to be a man, what it means to be God.[1]

And Buechner might have added, what it means to be an African Christian.

What this anonymous African artist has done is appropriate in several respects. In the words of the Letter to the Hebrews, Jesus is "the reflection of God's glory and the exact imprint of God's very being" (1:3), but he also became "like his brothers and sisters in every respect, so that he might be a merciful and faithful high priest in the service of God" (2:17). In the language of the Gospel according to John, Jesus is the Word made flesh, but not just flesh in general; rather, he is a particular flesh, a particular person. He has become like us in every respect, and we have every reason to imagine Jesus as "one of us," depending on who we understand the "us" to be. It was neither less nor more appropriate for this African artist to depict Jesus as an African than it was for a graphic artist named Warner Sallman in 1940 to depict the *Head of Christ* as a decidedly Western figure. Sallman's Jesus, wrote Stephen Prothero, "is movie-star perfect. His hair is flowing. And the light that baths his beautiful face begs to be described as dreamy."[2] By the beginning of the twenty-first century, this image of Jesus had been reproduced in 500 million copies. Both the anonymous African artist and Sallman were imagining Jesus as one "like [us] in every respect."

It is significant that the title of Buechner's book refers to the "faces" of Jesus. Jesus has as many faces as he does disciples. There is not one face to Jesus, and certainly not one correct face and many incorrect ones. It is striking how many books published during the last forty years use the metaphor of "face" as an organizing principle in constructive Christology. The term recognizes on the one hand the particularity of Jesus. Jesus is not any face, but a particular face, just as Jesus does not have followers in general but only specific followers. On the other hand, no one depiction of the face of Jesus can do justice to the cosmic Jesus, the Jesus who is Savior not just of specific people but also the Savior of the world, and who, therefore, is larger and more encompassing than every attempt to imagine him.[3]

The irony of the incarnation is that even though we are invited—perhaps even commanded—to imagine Jesus as one of us, nowhere does the New Testament describe what Jesus of Nazareth looked like. Was he tall or short, skinny or heavy, hairy or bald, handsome or ugly? The New Testament is strangely silent. It says nothing about Jesus' appearance or physical attributes, perhaps because it does indeed want its readers to imagine him as one of us, because the gospel is "for us and for our salvation" (Nicene Creed). It does depict Jesus, but it does so by describing what he says and does, how he relates to other people, and how in faith and obedience to the one he calls Abba, he responds to events that happen to him. Though the New Testament invites its readers to image (or to imagine) Jesus, it is important to remember that every depiction of him is necessary but insufficient. It is appropriate that we imagine him as like us "in every respect," but he is also unlike us in that his life is undistorted by sin. And one of the ways sin manifests itself in our lives, both individually and communally, is the way Christians have used their images of Jesus to justify their understanding of the world and to glorify themselves. In a patriarchal society it is hardly surprising that images of Jesus would emphasize his masculinity. Nor is it surprising in a free-market society based on consumption that Jesus' preferential option for the poor in Luke's Gospel would go largely unnoticed. When white Christians react negatively to the attempts of Africans, Asians, and Hispanics to depict Jesus as like them in every respect, they reveal more about themselves (and what they are) than they do about the faith of other people.

How Are Christians outside the West Contextualizing Jesus?

Historical criticism as a tool for interpreting the Bible has been important because it reminds contemporary Christians of the chasm between themselves and the Jesus of the first century. It serves as a check on our inclination to assume that our convictions about life and reality were shared by Jesus. At best we can be only partially aware of the historical and cultural assumptions we bring to the reading of the Bible and its descriptions of Jesus. No one (including this writer) reads the Bible without presuppositions, many of which are unconscious.

Even in Western Europe and North America many Christians read the Bible and understand Jesus differently because they have different life experiences and different assumptions about the world than those of the white males who traditionally have interpreted the meaning of the gospel. In the previous chapter we explored the importance of black history and culture in James Cone's reimagining of the black Christ. Black women, however, argued that Cone's first attempts at a theology that was no longer "white" reflected an unexamined patriarchy. "Womanist" theology, theology written from the perspective of black women, continues to emphasize the importance of Jesus as Liberator, but it is a Jesus who is relevant to black women's experience of both racism and sexism.[4] Delores Williams, for example, argues that a womanist Christology, rejecting the experience of "surrogacy" by many black women, should emphasize not the cross, which has too often been used to justify their continued self-denial and suffering, but the "ministerial vision" of Jesus.[5]

Christians who are neither white nor Western also read the Bible with different eyes and from perspectives shaped by their personal histories, the histories of their communities, and their racial and cultural locations. Many Christians in Africa and Asia, for example, live in cultures that, for different reasons in each case, emphasize the importance of family, the role of ancestors, and an affirmation of spirits and an unseen spiritual world. These are cultural realities that differ in important ways from the dominant cultures in Western Europe and North America, and not surprisingly, lead Christians in Africa and Asia to imagine the face of Jesus differently than have Christians in the West, for whom individualism has become more important than community, the present of more interest than the past, and for whom a "world come of age" (to use Bonhoeffer's phrase) has replaced a world of magic and mystery.

In both African and Asian interpretations of Christology, there is at least as much diversity as there is in Western interpretations. Just as it would be well nigh impossible to describe a consensus among Western Christians as to how Jesus should be understood, it is no less difficult to reduce African interpretations to a single point of view. Nonetheless, there are cultural images that many African theologians use in order to answer the question "Who is Jesus Christ for us today in Africa?" The images of Jesus as ancestor, chief, and healer are only a few that have emerged in African answers to this pivotal question. In his introduction to *Faces of Jesus in Africa*, Robert Schreiter observes that some of these African images and the values they reflect may actually be closer to the Bible than the images and values of Western Christianity: "The bitter irony, as African theologians have pointed out, is that African values and customs are often closer to the Semitic values that pervade the Scriptures and the story of Jesus than the European Christian values that have been imposed upon them."[6]

A case in point may be the importance in many African Christologies of the image of Jesus as ancestor and elder brother. While the commandment to "honor your father and your mother" may have fallen on sad days in the Western world, the use of the image of Jesus as ancestor by African Christians suggests that they may read and understand this commandment more appreciatively than Western Christians. In Bantu communities, ancestors are human beings who have lived especially worthy lives, given life, died natural deaths, and are now mediators between God and their descendants. They are not lost to the past but are present daily and can bless their descendants in matters of health, fertility, and prosperity.[7] It is not difficult to see why African Christians might be drawn to the image of Jesus as ancestor. It is Jesus who in John's Gospel has come "that they may have life, and have it abundantly" (10:10) and in Matthew's Gospel promises to be present "where two or three are gathered in my name" (18:20).

Asian Christians face challenges similar to those facing Christians in Africa and the rest of the world. They too have moved past the interpretation of the gospel first presented by Western missionaries and now search for images of Jesus that will make the gospel intelligible to their cultures. In addition, many of them find themselves in contexts where they are a distinct minority and cannot avoid the challenge of bringing Christian faith into conversation with much-larger and well-established religious communities, such as Hinduism, Buddhism, Confucianism, and Islam. How is Jesus similar to but different from Krishna, Buddha, Confucius, and Muhammad? Just as African Christians struggle to interpret Jesus in light of local cultural and religious traditions, so too Asian Christians have to find not only new images for Jesus, but also make sense of biblical claims about him in the context of non-Western interpretations of reality.

For example, Korean theologian Jung Young Lee has tried to reinterpret Christology by means of the *I Ching* rather than the traditional categories of Western metaphysics. "In Israel, as in all the ancient orient, in contrast to classical Greece, God's Word of utterance signified dynamic force, the power of change and transformation."[8] Consequently, Christ is the Word of God not as a form or structure, but as "the dynamic force that changes and produces new life and new possibilities."[9] In Jesus, therefore, there are no Western dualisms, no either/or. All things are reconciled and are not either/or but both/and. Lee uses the diagram of the Great Ultimate in the *I Ching* in which yin (darkness) and yang (light) are "interlocked but differentiated." The yin contains a yang, or light dot, and the yang contains a yin, or dark dot. As the light (yang) of the world, Christ includes darkness (yin), and yin (darkness) includes a dot of yang.

The relation between yin and yang might suggest a new way of understanding the relation between the two natures of Christ in classical Christianity. Using the language of God-consciousness, borrowed from Schleiermacher, Lee describes the enlargement of yang in the midst of yin as "a metaphor of the process of redemption or the growth of Christ-consciousness in us."[10] Yet another way of understanding Lee's proposal is as a form of the paradox that Paul develops in 1 Corinthians 15:10: "I worked harder than any of them—though it was not I, but the grace of God that is with me." In this model, sin would be the resistance to change; it is "the disruption of changing process and becoming," and salvation means "to follow the way of change without nostalgia."[11]

In Lee's Christology, Jesus is "the way of change, which is directed to the new creation."[12] Jesus "is *yang* and we are *yin*." By responding to yang, "we become creative, because *yin* becomes *yang* by response and *yang* becomes *yin* by creation."[13] Not surprisingly, salvation becomes something different from what it has been in Western Christianity. For Lee, it is "the harmony between the change and the changing or between the creator and the creature."[14] Christ is "the divine reality," the center of the changing process," in whom "all distinctions disappear." He is "the symbol of eternal change."[15]

Interpretations of Jesus as "ancestor" in African Christology or as "symbol of eternal change" in Asian theology are only the beginning, the first steps, of what will surely become a lengthy conversation among Christians in non-Western cultures as they search for language and paradigms that will enable Africans and Asians to confess Jesus as the Christ in their own cultural settings. There may be a time when it is appropriate for Western theologians to respond with questions and criticism, but initially it would be better if they simply listened and learned. What is inappropriate is the charge of "syncretism" occasionally made by

Western Christians. Syncretism can mean different things, but it is sometimes understood to be the uncritical combination or mixing of two or more opposed beliefs. It has sometimes been used in theology to describe the distortion of the gospel that results from accommodating it to convictions or practices from a non-Christian culture. What that use of the term seems to assume is either a "pure" Gospel that is somehow free from enculturation or a culture that is intrinsically Christian. Such a gospel and such a culture have never existed. The incarnation of the Word in Jesus of Nazareth is the primary instance of enculturation and syncretism. Not only did the Word become flesh; it also became a particular form of flesh in the person of a first-century Jewish male. Even in the classical Chalcedonian formula, the claim that two natures—one "fully God" and the other "fully human"—are united in one person is, as Kierkegaard described it, not only a paradox but also an "offense." The Christian claim that a first-century Jew is the Word made flesh is no less offensive than the claim that Jesus is ancestor or the symbol of eternal change.

Western Christians are sometimes blind to the many ways in which they have already enculturated the gospel. The mixing of the Christian celebration of the birth of Jesus with the figure of Santa Claus and the commercialization of both in Western capitalism, or the mixing of the Christian celebration of Christ's resurrection with spring fertility rites and bunny rabbits—these are only two of many ways in which Western Christianity has not only mixed the gospel with culture, but also seriously distorted it as well. A "successful" Christmas season in the West is often measured by retail sales. This is surely an egregious distortion of the gospel. Whatever Western theologians might say about interpretations of Jesus as the Christ in the non-Western world, syncretism is a charge best left unmentioned.

Who Is Jesus in Relation to the World's Religions?

Another major challenge facing theologians today is the relation of Jesus Christ to the other world religions. Not only must theologians in non-Western churches address the meaning of Jesus for their own cultures, but many of those cultures include religions such as Hinduism, Buddhism, and Islam. How are Christians to speak about their faith in Jesus Christ in conversation with Buddhist understandings of Siddhārtha Gautama, Hindu convictions about Krishna, Muslim beliefs about Muhammad, and Chinese interpretations of Confucius? Not only is religious pluralism a reality in many non-Western countries, but as we observed at the beginning of this chapter, it also is increasingly a fact of life in Western Europe and North America. It is a reality in almost every corner of the globe; even in those places where it is not a reality, most people encounter it on the Internet.

Some Christians respond to religious pluralism by pointing to numerous biblical texts that can be read as affirming the "finality" of Christ and seem to require people to believe that Jesus of Nazareth is the Christ, the Son of God, and the one Word of God in order to be saved. Many texts in John's Gospel are frequently read this way. Consider these verses: "For God so loved the world that he gave his only Son, so that everyone who believes in him may not perish but have eternal life" (3:16). "I am the gate. Whoever enters by me will be saved, and will come in and go out and find pasture" (10:9). "Jesus said to her, 'I am the resurrection and the life. Those who believe in me, even though they die, will live, and everyone who lives and believes in me will never die'" (11:25). "I am the way, and the truth, and the life. No one comes to the Father except through me" (14:6). In addition, perhaps the best-known New Testament text on the topic is Acts 4:12. Peter and John were arrested by Jewish leaders in Jerusalem and asked how they had been able to heal a man lame from birth. Peter, filled with the Holy Spirit, responded that the man was healed "by the name of Jesus Christ of Nazareth, whom you crucified, whom God raised from the dead. . . . There is salvation in no one else, for there is no other name under heaven given among mortals by which we must be saved" (4:10, 12).

Traditionally many (but not all) Christians have concluded from these texts and others that Jesus Christ is the only "Savior of the world" (John 4:42). Only those who confess faith in him can be saved. Some have also argued that there is no salvation apart from faith in him, and because the church is the body of Christ, there is no salvation outside the church. However, in the last half of the twentieth century, this position became increasingly difficult to sustain. As non-Christian religions ceased to be an abstraction and took the tangible form of neighbors and friends close at hand, as other religions assumed an individual and familiar face, it became increasingly difficult for Christians to dismiss their non-Christian neighbors as people who know nothing about the grace, mercy, and love of God. As Christians have observed the piety and spirituality of their non-Christian neighbors, many have come to respect what they had earlier dismissed and have concluded that there is much they can learn about God from those who have different names for God, different visions of God's face, and different understandings of God's reality.

During the latter third of the twentieth century, many theologians interpreted the relation between Christian faith and other faiths by means of a typology of exclusivism, inclusivism, and pluralism. Over the years these terms have meant different things to different theologians, but one way to interpret them is that exclusivists are those who hold that Jesus Christ is the one Word of God and the only way to salvation. Inclusivists, on the other hand, often affirm some form of theism or "theocentric" theology that makes room for a variety of different interpretations of God either by relativizing Christ, or by arguing that there are many manifestations of God's Word, or by arguing that non-Christians have encountered God's grace in Christ without realizing it. One version of the latter, for example, was the Roman Catholic theologian Karl Rahner's interpretation of some non-Christians as "anonymous Christians." Pluralists, unlike exclusivists, do not dismiss non-Christian faiths as false nor do they try to find a tent large enough to include all faiths. They simply acknowledge the reality of many different forms of faith and call for dialogue between them, a dialogue that recognizes their differences and affirms their distinctive features.

Many theologians now consider this typology too simple. Some religious faiths do not fit easily into any of these three types . Additionally, many theologians have argued that it may be the better part of wisdom not to begin a conversation between people of different faiths by talking about beliefs or truth claims. The issue of "truth" should be placed on the back burner, and religious dialogue should begin not with beliefs or doctrines but with the participants first trying to understand each other, to appreciate the other's faith as a daily experience. What are any given religion's sacred texts, core practices, forms of worship, moral values, religious holidays, food rituals, and understandings of reality? Those issues are initially more important for understanding a religious tradition than trying to assess the truth or falsity of its beliefs. Interreligious dialogue is more likely to have a future if the initial effort is to understand rather than trying to expose weaknesses and score debating points. Dialogue is something different from debate.

In the late 1970s a spirited debate about the relation between Christian faith and other religious traditions erupted with the publication of *The Myth of God Incarnate*, edited by John Hick (see chapter 5 above). Hick argued that in the new age of world ecumenism, Christians should acknowledge that classical Christology, represented by the Council of Nicaea in the fourth century and Chalcedon in the fifth, the first and fourth ecumenical councils (see chapter 3), is not eternal truth, but "only one way of conceptualizing the lordship of Jesus." It is also both optional and mythological.[16] There are multiple ways of interpreting the meaning of Christ, even within the New Testament. Furthermore, the world has moved beneath the church's feet, and a new situation has emerged in which it is no longer possible for Christians to approach other faiths with an agenda of conversion. The church's task has fundamentally changed: "We have to present Jesus and the Christian life in a way compatible with our new recognition of the validity of the other great world faiths as being also, at their best, ways of salvation."[17]

When Christians claimed that there was no way to salvation apart from Jesus Christ, many assumed that everyone agreed on what "salvation" means. However, a quick look at the Bible suggests that it contains multiple interpretations of salvation. Is salvation physical healing or the exorcism of demons? Or is it not only the physical and psychological healing of people but also the mending of an endangered creation that now groans in travail? Is it a turning around and a recovery of life lived before God? Is it the forgiveness of sins? Or is it singing eternal praise, unending doxology, to God?

Furthermore, in conversation with non-Christians it quickly becomes apparent that other religions have quite different interpretations of salvation than do Christians, if they use the category at all. In Buddhism, for example, salvation has more to do with enlightenment than the forgiveness of sins. Because different religions have different interpretations of the goal of the religious life, the question whether one must have faith in Jesus as the Christ in order to be "saved" is beside the point if there is no agreement on what the human problem is, on what constitutes human salvation, and whether salvation is a relevant category.

And the world's religions have different understandings not only of "salvation," but also of such basic concepts as "God." Christians sometimes forget that their understanding of theism is not shared by some other religious traditions. Even the so-called "monotheistic religions" differ strongly on whether the one God is triune.

Even if Christians could find some basis for agreement with other religions on terms such as "salvation" and "God," Hick argues that Christianity must change its entire way of thinking about these issues. If Christianity is to engage other religions, it must first move beyond what he describes as its "theological fundamentalism," by which he means "its literal interpretation of the idea of incarnation." The story "of the Son of God coming down from heaven and being born as a baby," Hick argues, is mythology and must not be taken literally, because if understood literally it becomes impossible for Christians to have genuine dialogue with people of other faiths. If Christians enter that conversation presupposing that Jesus Christ is the only way to God, the conversation can only be a monologue and never a genuine dialogue.

As far as Hick is concerned, the classical doctrine of the incarnation is no longer viable. He recasts Jesus as "intensely and overwhelmingly conscious of the reality of God," as "so powerfully God-conscious that his life vibrated, as it were, to the divine life."

If we had been in Jesus' presence, "we should have felt that we are in the presence of God—not in the sense that the man Jesus literally *is* God, but in the sense that he was so totally conscious of God that we could catch something of that consciousness by spiritual contagion." In a later book, Hick further developed his Christology by arguing that Christians should understand the incarnation metaphorically. But even when understood metaphorically, Jesus remains, for Hick, "a man living in a startling degree of awareness of God and of response to God's presence."[18] As we noted in chapter 5, Schleiermacher's interpretation of Jesus' perfect God-consciousness has been remarkably influential in contemporary Christology.

Hick argued that if Christians want to enter into genuine dialogue with people of other faiths, they must give up their "absolute" claims about Jesus Christ. He was by no means the first to argue that Christian claims to absolute truth raise a number of difficult problems. From Ernst Troeltsch at the beginning of the twentieth century to postmodernists at its close, numerous questions have been raised about any claim to universal and absolute truth. As philosophers and theologians became increasingly aware that human knowledge is always relative to the historical and social location of the knower and that no human being has access to some Archimedean point outside of history, all claims to absolute knowledge seemed to be relativized. That development means that no one, including Christians, holds a position that enables them to make an objective comparison of conflicting truth claims. Christians might make confessional, as opposed to universal, claims about the importance of God's self-disclosure in Jesus Christ, but they have no basis for evaluating non-Christian truth claims.

Furthermore, Christian claims to knowledge of absolute truth make conversation with people of other faiths increasingly difficult. If Christians begin that conversation by assuming that they alone know God's saving grace, the only point to the discussion, from their point of view, is to enable others to see the error of their ways. From that perspective, Christians have nothing to learn about God from non-Christian faiths. The only point to the dialogue is to enlighten the other.

There are two large theological problems with that point of view. First, it identifies Jesus Christ with what Christians believe about him. For several reasons that seems to be an unwise assumption. Christians believe that Jesus Christ has been raised and lives and is not a historical artifact that belongs in a museum. Consequently Christian claims about Jesus Christ can at best be only provisional because his story is unfinished. He still "will come again in glory to judge the quick and the dead" (Nicene Creed): all the living and the dead, including faithful Christians. Jesus Christ, therefore, can no more be confined to anyone's dogma or theology than he could to the tomb of Joseph of Arimathea. It is important not to confuse Christ and Christianity. The two are not the same. Christian theology is a thoroughly human interpretation of the meaning and significance of Jesus. It is one thing to say, with John's Gospel, that Jesus Christ is "the way, and the truth, and the life" (John 14:6); it is something else to say that any theological interpretation of Jesus is also the way, the truth, and the life. Christian theology is at best an imperfect, fallible discipline that will always be provisional and in need of correction.

A second theological problem with Christian claims about absolute truth is that it seems to deny the reality and work of the Holy Spirit. According to the New Testament, there are many different spirits in the world, and in order to discern which is God's Spirit, Christians should ask whether a spirit is the Spirit of Jesus Christ (1 John 4:1–3). That is, does the Spirit promote love rather than hate, does it reconcile rather than estrange, does it build up rather than tear down? Just as Christ is not the captive of any particular church or theology, so too Christ's Spirit moves where it wills. It is not confined or restricted to the walls of any church or the theology of any denomination.

That means that Christians should approach serious, honest conversation with other faiths not as a sporting contest in which someone will win and the other will lose, but in eager anticipation that they might encounter the living Christ and his Spirit in other people and other faiths. Christians do not take Christ to the rest of the world. Just as Christ's Spirit is at work in the world wherever life appears, where new life emerges from death, and wherever there is freedom, so too Christ is present in the world and calls the church to be where he is already at work. Understood in these terms, it may be that Christians receive more than they give in interreligious dialogue. Interreligious dialogue, then, is not an exercise of Christian benevolence toward non-Christians, but an opportunity for the continuing growth, edification, transformation, and sanctification of Christians. Other faiths are not a problem to be solved, an obstacle to be overcome, an enemy to be defeated, but an opportunity for Christians to grow in their faith in a Christ who is always larger than their theologies and greater than their imaginations.

Who Is Jesus Christ in a Pluralist, Postmodern World?

Religious pluralism is a fact of life. People in the United States no longer live in a "Christian" nation and probably never did. There are those who think that the vaguely defined term "postmodernism" is a passing fad. It may be, but the reality of pluralism and all the issues it raises are not. If the term refers to a society that is no longer homogenous (if it ever was); a society in which there is no longer a defining center, either in terms of "master narratives" or moral and political values; a society in which traditional norms are continually being called into question—then in that broad sense of the term, we live in the midst of postmodernism. Some thinkers decry this development. They fear that it points to a future in which all values are relativized, with moral nihilism and social anarchy just around the corner. On the other hand, it is at least conceivable that these destabilizing social developments are the work of a destabilizing Spirit of God and point to a future in which the world's diversity will better resemble the creation that God intends.

Should Christians fear pluralism? There is good reason to think that they should not. One could argue that pluralism is built into the very structure of Christian faith. The Christian conviction that God is triune, that the divine life consists of three names who are distinct but inseparable, and who in their relations to one another constitute one reality—this conviction points to a pluralism of sorts within the very being of God. So too it is perhaps providential and by no means accidental that the New Testament contains four different Gospels that point to one Christ. No single Gospel is sufficient to express the full mystery and reality of the Christ. Not only does John's Gospel differ significantly from that of the Synoptic Gospels (Mark, Matthew, and Luke), but they also differ in important ways in their interpretations of Jesus. For example, they all agree that Jesus was crucified, but their descriptions of "the last words" of Jesus point to quite different interpretations of his death and therein different interpretations of what it means to say he is the Christ.

Finally, there is good reason—in the witness of Scripture—to believe that neither Christians nor anyone else will ever understand the full glory of Christ until all things—all of creation—finally stand before him and sing doxology.

Notes

Chapter 1: Does Christ Matter?

1. Flannery O'Connor, *Wise Blood* (New York: Noonday Press, 1962), 105.
2. Paul Tillich, *Systematic Theology*, vol. 2, *Existence and the Christ* (Chicago: University of Chicago Press, 1957), 97–98.
3. The Nicene Creed, in *Book of Confessions: Study Edition* (Louisville, KY: Geneva Press, 1996), 9 (1.2).
4. The Confession of 1967, in *Book of Confessions: Study Edition*, 322 (9.08).
5. Dietrich Bonhoeffer, *Letters and Papers from Prison*, ed. Eberhard Bethge, enlarged ed. (New York: Macmillan, 1971), 279.
6. Philipp Melanchthon, *Loci communes theologici*, trans. Lowell J. Satre and Wilhelm Pauck, in *Melanchthon and Bucer*, ed. Wilhelm Pauck, Library of Christian Classics 19 (Philadelphia: Westminster Press, 1969), 21.
7. Ibid., 22.
8. The Nicene Creed, in *Book of Confessions: Study Edition*, 9 (1.2).
9. Flannery O'Connor, "A Good Man Is Hard to Find," in *The Complete Stories* (New York: Farrar, Straus & Giroux, 1971), 132.
10. John Calvin, *Institutes of the Christian Religion*, ed. John T. McNeill, trans. Ford Lewis Battles (Philadelphia: Westminster Press, 1960), 494–503 (2.15).
11. Augustine of Hippo, *Confessions*, trans. R. S. Pine-Coffin (London: Penguin Books, 1961), 207.
12. Theological Declaration of Barmen, in *Book of Confessions: Study Edition*, 311 (8.17).

Chapter 2: Who Was Jesus, Really?

1. T. S. Eliot, "East Coker," in "Four Quartets," in *The Complete Poems and Plays, 1909–1950* (New York: Harcourt, Brace & World, 1962), 123, 129.
2. The Confession of 1967, in *Book of Confessions: Study Edition*, 322 (9.08).

3. Eduard Schweizer, *Jesus*, trans. David E. Green (Richmond, VA: John Knox Press, 1971), 16.

Chapter 3: How Is Jesus "Savior"?

1. Calvin, *Institutes of the Christian Religion*, 494–503 (2.15).
2. A Brief Statement of Faith, in *Book of Confessions: Study Edition*, 342 (lines 23–26).
3. T. S. Eliot, choruses from "The Rock," in *The Complete Poems and Plays*, 110.
4. C. S. Lewis, *Mere Christianity* (New York: Macmillan Co., 1960), 42.
5. A Declaration of Faith, in *Our Confessional Heritage: Confessions of the Reformed Tradition with a Contemporary Declaration of Faith* (Atlanta: Materials Distribution Service, The Presbyterian Church in the United States, 1978), 180 (line 89).
6. The Scots Confession, in *Book of Confessions: Study Edition*, 33 (3.01).
7. Theological Declaration of Barmen, in *Book of Confessions: Study Edition*, 311 (8.11).

Chapter 4: What Did the Early Christians Believe about Jesus?

1. For a fuller discussion of this material, see J. N. D. Kelly, *Early Christian Doctrines* (New York: Harper & Row, 1960); or Frances M. Young, *From Nicaea to Chalcedon: A Guide to the Literature and Its Background* (Philadelphia: Fortress Press, 1983).
2. The Chalcedonian Decree, in *Christology of the Later Fathers*, ed. Edward Rochie Hardy, Library of Christian Classics 3 (Philadelphia: Westminster Press, 1954), 373.
3. G. K. Chesterton, *Orthodoxy* (New York: Doubleday & Co., 1959), 92.
4. *Søren Kierkegaard's Journals and Papers*, ed. Howard V. Hong and Edna H. Hong, vol. 1 (Bloomington: Indiana University Press, 1967), 125.
5. John Calvin, The Catechism of the Church of Geneva, in *Our Confessional Heritage*, 23 (#55).
6. The Confession of 1967, in *Book of Confessions: Study Edition*, 322 (9.08).
7. A Declaration of Faith, in *Our Confessional Heritage*, 163 (lines 23–48).
8. Ibid., 162 (lines 14–22).

Chapter 5: What Are People Today Saying about Jesus?

1. Friedrich Schleiermacher, *The Christian Faith*, ed. H. R. Macintosh and J. S. Stewart (Philadelphia: Fortress Press, 1977), 374–475.
2. John Hick, ed., *The Myth of God Incarnate* (Philadelphia: Westminster Press, 1977), 167–185.
3. Albrecht Ritschl, *The Christian Doctrine of Justification and Reconciliation*, trans. H. R. Mackintosh and A. R. Macaulay (Clifton, NJ: Reference Book Publishers, 1966), 385–484.

4. Rudolf Bultmann, "On the Question of Christology," in *Faith and Understanding I*, trans. Louise Pettibone Smith (New York: Harper & Row, 1969), 116–44.
5. Edward Schillebeeckx, *Jesus: An Experiment in Christology*, trans. Hubert Hoskins (New York: Seabury Press, 1979); and idem, *Christ: The Experience of Jesus as Lord*, trans. John Bowden (New York: Seabury Press, 1979).
6. Jon Sobrino, *Christology at the Crossroads: A Latin American Approach* (Maryknoll, NY: Orbis Books, 1978); idem, *Jesus the Liberator* (Maryknoll, NY: Orbis Books, 1993); idem, *Christ the Liberator* (Maryknoll, NY: Orbis Books, 2001).
7. James H. Cone, *God of the Oppressed* (New York: Seabury Press, 1975), 137.
8. Wolfhart Pannenberg, *Jesus—God and Man*, trans. Lewis L. Wilkins and Duane A. Priebe (Philadelphia: Westminster Press, 1968), 53–114; and *Systematic Theology*, vol. 2 (Grand Rapids: Wm. B. Eerdmans Pub. Co., 1994), 277–464.
9. Pannenberg, *Systematic Theology*, 2:363.
10. Ibid., 281.
11. Ibid., 304.
12. Ibid., 303.
13. Ibid., 398.
14. Jürgen Moltmann, *Theology of Hope: On the Ground and the Implications of a Christian Eschatology*, trans. James W. Leitch (London: SCM, 1967).
15. Jürgen Moltmann, *The Crucified God: The Cross of Christ as the Foundation and Criticism of Christian Theology* (London: SCM Press, 1974).
16. Jürgen Moltmann, *The Way of Jesus Christ: Christology in Messianic Dimensions*, trans. Margaret Kohl (San Francisco: HarperSanFrancisco, 1990).
17. Ibid., 73.
18. Ibid., 213–15.
19. Ibid., 214.
20. Mary Daly, *Beyond God the Father: Toward a Philosophy of Women's Liberation* (Boston: Beacon Press, 1973), 19.
21. Rosemary Radford Ruether, "Christology: Can a Male Savior Save Women?" in *Sexism and God-Talk: Toward a Feminist Theology* (Boston, Beacon Press, 1983), 116–38.
22. Ibid., 13.
23. Ibid., 18–19.
24. Ibid., 23.
25. Ibid., 24.
26. Ibid., 131.
27. Ibid., 138.
28. Elizabeth A. Johnson, *She Who Is: The Mystery of God in Feminist Theological Discourse* (New York: Crossroad, 1992), 32.
29. Ibid., 156.
30. Ibid., 161–63.

31. James H. Cone, *A Black Theology of Liberation*, 2nd ed. (Maryknoll, NY: Orbis Books, 1986), 111.
32. Karl Barth, *Church Dogmatics*, trans. G. W. Bromiley (Edinburgh: T&T Clark, 1956–58), IV/1:157–357 and IV/2:3–377.
33. H. Richard Niebuhr, *The Meaning of Revelation* (New York: Macmillan, 1940).
34. Hans Frei, *The Identity of Jesus Christ: The Hermeneutical Bases of Dogmatic Theology* (Philadelphia: Fortress Press, 1975).
35. Ibid., 126–38.

Chapter 6: Who Is Jesus Christ in a Pluralistic World?

1. Frederick Buechner, *The Faces of Jesus*, photography by Lee Boltin, design by Ray Ripper (1974; New York: Stearn / Harper & Row, 1989), 172.
2. Stephen Prothero, *American Jesus: How the Son of God Became a National Icon* (New York: Farrar, Straus & Giroux, 2003), 119.
3. For example, see Robert J. Schreiter, ed., *Faces of Jesus in Africa* (Maryknoll, NY: Orbis Books, 1991); R. S. Sugirtharajah, ed., *Asian Faces of Jesus* (Maryknoll, NY: Orbis Books, 1993); and Volker Küster, *The Many Faces of Jesus Christ: Intercultural Christology* (Maryknoll, NY: Orbis Books, 2001). That all of these books are published by Orbis Books suggests a theological commitment on the part of its editors.
4. See Jacquelyn Grant, *White Women's Christ and Black Woman's Jesus* (Atlanta: Scholars Press, 1989); and her essay "'Come to My Help, Lord, For I'm in Trouble': Womanist Jesus and the Mutual Struggle for Liberation," in *Reconstructing the Christ Symbol: Essays in Feminist Theology*, ed. Maryanne Stevens (New York: Paulist Press, 1993), 54–71.
5. Delores S. Williams, *Sisters in the Wilderness: The Challenge of Womanist God-Talk* (Maryknoll, NY: Orbis Books, 1993), 143–77.
6. Schreiter, *Faces of Jesus in Africa*, viii.
7. See François Kabasélé's essay "Christ as Ancestor and Elder Brother," in ibid., 116–27.
8. Jung Young Lee, "The Perfect Realization of Change: Jesus Christ," in Sugirtharajah, *Asian Faces of Jesus*, 64.
9. Ibid.
10. Ibid., 66.
11. Ibid., 67
12. Ibid.
13. Ibid., 68.
14. Ibid.
15. Ibid., 70.
16. Hick, *Myth of God Incarnate*, 168.
17. Ibid., 182.
18. John Hick, *The Metaphor of God Incarnate: Christology in a Pluralistic Age*, 2nd ed. (Louisville, KY: Westminster John Knox Press, 2005), 106.